COLLEGE 101

THE BOOK YOUR COLLEGE DOES NOT WANT YOU TO READ

By
Guy Stevens
Third Edition
The Back Alley Press

College 101: The Book Your College Does Not Want You To Read

By Guy Stevens

Published By:

The Back Alley Press
10941 Vallerosa Street
Las Vegas, NV 89141
781-785-4000

First Printing 1997

Second Printing 1999, revised

Third Printing 2004, revised

04 10 9 8 7 6 5 4

ISBN 0-9664122-1-4

Artwork Acknowledgements
Original Artwork Created by Enrique "Zeke" Savory JR.

Trademark Acknowledgements

Table Of Contents

DISCLAIMER

The publisher, author, The Back Alley Press, or its parent company The Back Alley Media LLC, assume no responsibility for the material presented in this book entitled, College 101 : The Book You College Does Not Want You To Read. Although every effort has been made to insure the accuracy and validity of the material presented, the reader or purchaser assumes all responsibility for the use of the material.

DISCLAIMER

THE ADVENTURES OF GUY STEVENS
RECOVERING COLLEGE STUDENT
CITY COLLEGE
At a secret meeting in the dean's office...
Mr. Stevens the college feels that it would be in your best interest...
...Not To Publish THIS MANUSCRIPT
But- - The Truth Must Be Told!
NO !
The TRUTH is what we say it is. This book will never see light of day...
We'll see about that!

ACME PUBLISHING
BIG TIME PRESS INC.
XYZ PUBLISHIN
I'm sorry but ACME Publishing just isn't interested in your book.
You want Big Time Press to publish this? You're joking... right?.
XYZ Publishing doesn't publish manuscripts that might be deemed "controversial". We value our relationship with City College.
Meanwhile...evil forces conspire!
My rent is due. I don't have a job. I'm broke.
Ring Ring
Guy Stevens - I want to see YOU!
At the office of The Back Alley Press!
This is EXACTLTY the kind of manuscript I have been looking for. It will make all the right people very upset!

Publisher's Note

As a publisher, I am always plagued with frustration: It is hard to find manuscripts that are really worth publishing. All too often I run across authors who try to be too politically correct. They have no point of view and simply fail to provide compelling information. Given the glut of books on just about any topic on the market, it must be hard for the reader, too, to pick out those that are any good and worth reading.

When I accepted College 101, I knew that there are too many "cute" college guides around, written, it appears, by perky former sorority sisters, whose biggest collegial dilemma consisted of choosing between a stripling blue blood and the son of an oil baron for the next formal dance. But does anybody really want to read about the perfect little college experience? Oh yawn!

One popular so-called college guide, written by an octogenarian sex therapist, does a brisk business. Another book claims to have 101 insights that you should know before you go to college. Upon closer inspection, however, it becomes clear that the alleged wisdom behind the advice in this book is nothing but a crock of bull. Obviously, the author needs to be knocked down a few notches. So for your pleasure, here is some of her profound advice with Guy Steven's corrective comments:

"**Heartily greet and thank the cafeteria workers**" - Why? So I can thank them for the extra 15 pounds I packed on? So I can thank them for the awful mystery matter they claimed was meatloaf? So I can thank them for making me starve on liver night?

"**Don't be afraid to cry**" - Is this advice for before or after I receive my tuition bill?

"**Smile at everyone on campus**" - This would remove all doubts that I escaped from a mental institution!

"**Be prepared to change your major 27 times**" - Why would I like wasting money?

"**Write thank-you notes for everything**" - Dear Professor, thanks for the failing grade. I really appreciated it. Please let me know if I can return the favor.

just don't get it! What does an octogenarian sex therapist know about the modern college experience? These guidebooks are a fraud on the reading public. They are just another one in the long string of rip-offs college students must guard against! These books do not offer solutions. In fact, they themselves are part of the problem!

By contrast, what I like about Guy Stevens' account is that he reveals the mistakes he has made-many of them. He took his share of hard knocks and learned from them. His manuscript reveals all the secrets of his college experience-warts and all-and he reveals them with a healthy dose of detachment, with plenty of humor, and with an appropriate amount of irreverence, sarcasm, and cynicism.

While Guy will never win a Pulitzer Prize for his college stories, he should be commended for poking the seedy underbelly of the so-called institutions of higher learning. Believe it or not, those glossy college brochures and those happy recruitment videos do lie! What they leave out is the true reality of college life: insensitive bureaucracy, dilapidated student housing, buffoon professors, and eye-gouging prices at the campus convenience stores.

The Back Alley Press is an independent publishing company dedicated to the motto of "giving a voice to those who might not otherwise get one." In a world of vast media consolidation we'd like to think that we can still make a difference. We try to be the champion of the "the little guy." We only publish manuscripts with an axe to grind or a bone to pick. We do not suck up to the establishment. This is why we feel strongly that College 101 is a fitting addition to our publishing program.

We hope you'll enjoy College 101. May you find it both entertaining and informative.

President
The Back Alley Press

Introduction

Every year, once the new freshmen have arrived on campus, they must endure the same tired old speech that begins: "Look to your left. Look to your right. Some of you won't be here at the end of four years." It is the classic "scare-the-freshmen-into-studying "speech-inevitably delivered by some stuffy old dean or university president who hasn't seen daylight for the past ten years.

Just as the above scene is a classic college cliché, so is the material contained in many college guides that fill the shelves of college bookstores. Rarely do these guides give you sage advice or tell you the tales of woe that can only come from real experiences by real people. The truth is that most of these guides are written by staff writers, who are way beyond their college years and who work for publishing companies that are more interested in filling a gap in their publishing program than in disseminating useful information. Seems to me that these so-called guides do more harm than good to the intended reader.

Sometimes college can seem as twisted as an old Warner Brothers cartoon, especially after you have had your inevitable and disheartening encounters with incompetent college bureaucrats, unreasonable professors, greedy campus bookstores, obnoxious pranksters, rip-off artists, and screwy roommates. Atrocious high-fat, high-calorie cafeteria food, unfair exams, and broken-down washing machines don't make every-day college life cheery either. Fortunately, this book will tell you everything you need to know to avoid these problems-or at least to cope with them-so that you may have the most productive four years possible, given the sometimes dismal circumstances in which you are likely to find yourself during your college career.

One reviewer claimed: "I would be concerned that students reading this book will get an unrealistically negative impression of the college experience, and they might go to college expecting (and looking for) deception and malice, which might be demoralizing." Well, reality may be demoralizing, but is that a reason to suppress it? I'd rather think of my point of view as a George Carlinesque swipe at the college industry. And make no mistake: College is an industry, not a charitable institution! By illustrating my mistakes, my follies, and my triumphs, I hope I can give you a few "street smarts" and thus make you a better player in the game of college survival.

I have seen firsthand ALL the craziness college has to offer. Not only have I dealt with uncouth roommates, a corrupt student government, and exams from hell, I also went through the joys of college life in a forbidding climate that caused my nose hairs to freeze. As if that wasn't bad enough, I once had to drop three floors from a window, using a rope tied to a bed frame, to escape a deranged lunatic who had barricaded my dorm room door shut. Plain and simple, I hope to give you the book colleges would rather you not read!

Guy Stevens
Recovering College Student

CHAPTER 1
THE DORMITORY

One of my fondest college memories is of the freshman residence hall, a complex affectionately called *The Pit* by its inmates. It was one of the older dorms on campus, with a long history of rowdy freshman living. It wasn't much to look at, but it soon became home.

Because most colleges do not allow freshmen to live in off-campus apartments, you will probably find yourself living in a freshman dormitory room. When you are not in class, the library, or the dining hall, that's the place where you'll probably be. It will not be much larger than a prison cell and it will require effort to turn it into a home. And that's not all. You probably won't have the room to yourself.

ROOM OCCUPANCY

Dormitory rooms generally come in the form of single, double, or triple occupancy. In some colleges, you may even be placed in a "quad" (four occupants to a room). The campus housing office will most likely offer you a choice. I strongly advise against a quad or triple, because, in a quad, arguments between four roommates can lead to deadlocks, and in a triple, as the old saying goes, "Two's company, three's a crowd." With an uneven number of roommates, in a disagreement, it is usually two against one...and you don't want to be the odd person out. Therefore, let's just consider the advantages and disadvantages of single and double dorm rooms.

SINGLE OCCUPANCY

Advantages

Privacy will never be an issue, because you have the entire room to yourself. Peace and quiet will prevail, when you need to study.

Disadvantages

Single rooms are usually more expensive. The lack of companionship may make it harder to make new friends. Unless you have a magnetic personality, people may not walk into your room to meet you.

DOUBLE OCCUPANCY

Advantages

A roommate could become an instant ally and friend. The two of you can share expenses and be study partners. A roommate may be able to provide furnishings and appliances so you don't have to purchase them. Lastly, a roommate can act as your secretary and take your phone messages.

Disadvantages

A roommate can quickly turn from new best friend into your worst enemy. This same person could steal money from you, mistreat your personal property, and be insensitive to your needs. In the worst possible scenario, this person could be an alcoholic, a drug user, or prone to violence.

I hate to admit it, but I had a few terrible roommates. I have lived with drug users, vampires, wackos and weirdos! In fact I once lived with a guy who was so paranoid that he used to lock up his cooking utensils for the night because he feared I might steal them. (Why on earth would I want to steal somebody's frying pan!) This same asylum escapee made sure that none of my food touched his food because he thought my germs would contaminate his food! When I finally moved into a single room, things got better: my sanity improved and my grade-point average (GPA) went from 2.7 to 3.725.

My advice about roommates, therefore, comes down to this: During your freshman year, try to get a double room. Make all your friends then so that, in your sophomore year (or junior year, at the latest), you can get a single room.

BEFORE TAKING A DOUBLE ROOM

Read the housing questionnaire carefully and answer all questions honestly. This will make it more likely that you will get a good roommate match. You will be required to answer such questions as: Do you smoke? Do you have any allergies? What is your gender? (This is particularly meaningful if you have a unisex name like Kelly, Chris, or B.J.)

Try to select a roommate with the same major as yours so you can study and work on projects together. Before you arrive on campus, contact your roommate, to try to get to know him/her a little. Find out what he or she is bringing so that you don't duplicate such items as a TV or a stereo set. Ask which kind of music he/she likes, whether he/she is a night owl, and how he/she feels about parties.

Lastly, find out if there is a girl- or boyfriend? Might your roommate have casual, overnight guests? If your roommate-to-be has a significant other, a few scenarios could come into play. Your double could suddenly turn into a triple! In other words, you might have an additional roommate with whom you may not get along. It may be the case that your roommate will never be home because he/she is at the significant other's place. Or, you may have to spend time away from your room whenever your roommate wants to be intimate with someone. You probably do not want to spend your nights in the hallway merely for your roommate's pleasure!

In spite of all your precautions in selecting a roommate, things can still go wrong. I know that I was not always prefect at this game. I learned that some of my classmates made great study partners but horrible roommates.

Roommate issues are very common on campus. A friend of mine once told me her little tale of woe: "Never choose your roommate at freshman orientation as I once did. Initially I thought she was really nice and we seemed to have a lot in common. I suggested that we room together. Unfortunately, after living with her for a while, I realized we had little in common. She had really bad mood swings–one minute she was really friendly, the next minute she was making odd noises or slamming the door and not saying good bye when she left. She even ate my food!"

THE ROOM

FURNISHINGS

Once you've decided on your rooming option, you'll want to concentrate on the room itself. Dormitory rooms are far from deluxe accommodations. But no matter what, certain furnishings are common to most dorm rooms. Usually there is a bed, desk, closet and chest of drawers for each resident. Rudimentary lighting, a bookshelf, and a mirror

make up the rest of the furnishings.

Space is at a premium. In four years' time, however, you will become an expert at squeezing tons of stuff into tiny spaces. In the section "Decorating Your Room" below and in chapter 2, I will discuss furnishings and what you can do to personalize them. But first let's look at what the housing office expects of you at the time you take *possession* of your room, and what they want it to look like when you return it at the end of your tenancy.

Damages

Upon your first arrival on campus, the housing office most likely will give you a room damage report. Considering that you will be living in this room for nearly eight months, give real consideration to the issue of room damages. The report asks you to look over all furniture, fixtures, and walls in your room and to write down any noticeable damage. By filling out this form, you are supposedly protected from being billed at the end of the year for any preexisting room damage. Be very thorough. The last thing you want is to be billed for damage you didn't cause.

My own experience with room damage has taught me that it's nearly impossible not to be billed for something. In my opinion, many campus housing authorities use phony room damages as an excuse to get additional money out of students.

My favorite room damage scam dealt with corkboards. My freshman room had a white corkboard. The moment I put a tack into the corkboard I had perpetrated the heinous crime of room damage. The evil housing office claimed that the corkboard needed to be repainted at the end of the year. I was billed for this! (I thought the whole purpose of having a corkboard was to use tacks!) In hindsight, I should have fought the charge. Don't let your housing authority scam you into paying for these trumped-up charges!

Of course, if you feel you have been railroaded, you can always consult a higher authority. (If your parents are footing the tuition bill, they are a higher authority!) When a friend of mine received a highly overstated room damages invoice demanding a ridiculous sum for repainting the room, his father complained and, bingo, the price went down.

If for some reason you don't like the color scheme in your room, **don't repaint it**, because, if you do, you'll just have to paint it again in the original color at the end of the school year (or semester if you change rooms mid-year). And if you don't use the exact original color, or if you do a poor job, you'll have to pay the college to repaint it, so you'll be out not only your cost for paint, but also their (inflated) cost for paint and labor.

Before leaving your room at the end of the year, make sure you repair any holes you might have made in the walls, especially if you hung pictures or had a dartboard. Some people swear by using toothpaste for this cover-up job, but I've never had any luck with it. I've tried every method of filling holes, and the best thing I've found is spackle. You can find spackle and a disposable putty knife at any hardware store.

The housing office didn't always win in battle against me! One year I had a hole in my wall that was much too large for a cosmetic job. My next-door neighbor had chiseled through the wall from his room into mine, creating a six-inch hole. I stuffed paper towels and newspaper into the hole, then smeared spackle over it. He did the same on his side. To this day neither of us has been billed for the hole. I went back to the old room a few times to check on the hole. As far as I know the patch is still in place.

If you are the type of person who likes to plaster a room with posters, **don't use tape**. All tape, Scotch, masking, and even duct, will peal the paint when removed. The very worst type of tape is the double-sided variety. It sticks really well, but you can't get it off either the wall or the poster. Your best bet for avoiding room damage is to use FunTack , a clay-like substance made specifically for hanging posters and pictures. It comes off both the wall and the poster effortlessly.

I once bought a roll of double-sided tape. It vanished within hours. When I found the empty roll lying on a counter top, I asked where all the tape had gone. My roommate pointed to the ceiling. I couldn't believe my eyes. He had taped all the desk lamps, empty beer bottles, and various other items to the ceiling. It was actually pretty cool to look at but an absolute horror to remove.

DECORATING

Once you have filled out the room damage report, you are ready to arrange the furniture and to make it as comfortable as your limited time and means allow. Try to make the best use of the available space. Functionally, you want every inch to count, but personalizing the room is just as important. After all, your dorm room is probably your first living environment that is uniquely yours, that reflects your personality and your interests. Mom and Dad won't be able to stop you from plastering the walls with posters or drilling holes. Your freedom to decorate is limited only by your creativity and the weight of your wallet.

It is likely that you and your roommate(s) will not have exactly the same tastes–you may not like the same bands, movies, politicians, actors, or scenery. Therefore, you should quickly mark off who gets to decorate which areas. Remember that there are four walls, one or more windows, a ceiling, a floor, a door (not to mention a closet door), and the hallway (although the latter may have to be shared with other hall residents).

The furniture the college provides for dorm rooms is usually a tad Spartan. A couch, coffee table, easy chair, or even a beanbag can make the room more bearable. These and other items you can find at yard sales and in thrift shops. Of course, you can bring them from home, but I recommend buying them after you get on campus, when you know how much or how little space you've got to work with.

Sometimes students have decorating aspirations beyond their means. As the old saying goes, "Champagne taste on a beer budget." One group of enterprising classmates solved that problem in a most ingenious way. They piled into a pickup truck, drove to the state college down the road. They walked into the student lounge and loaded all its furniture into the pickup truck. That evening one particular dorm room had rather extravagant furnishings. Campus security was not pleased. Although I do not condone these student's actions, I do admire their ingenuity!

The ceiling is often overlooked as a space with decorating potential. You could leave it blank, but that wouldn't be half the fun. Dangle a mobile or two. Put up glow-in-the-dark stars. (This will make your ceiling into a galaxy when you turn out the lights at night.) Drape fishnets. (I don't know if there's a practical purpose for doing this, but it looks cool.) Hang posters. (Contrary to popular opinion, posters are just as effective on ceilings as they are on vertical surfaces.) If you really want to freak people out, attach bottles and other objects to the ceiling to create a pseudo-upside-down room.

Use creative lighting to give blank walls texture. Strobe, Christmas tree, or black lights, road-hazard flashers, plasma spheres, lava lamps, and disco balls can do wonders. I find lava lamps both hypnotic and attention-grabbing.

CAUTION: Road hazard flashers can get you into trouble. Never steal these from local construction sites. One enterprising student I knew "borrowed" one from a small excavation site near his campus and put it in his window. Within a few nights, campus security showed up and demanded to know where it came from.

Don't overlook the refrigerator as a surface to decorate. Use magnets to attach pictures, restaurant menus, and notes with important phone numbers. Decorative magnets such as letters of the alphabet and *magnetic poetry kits* can add fun.

Your window(s) can provide a big chance for the proverbial "fifteen minutes of fame." Hang Christmas lights, your collection of beer cans, and weird pictures there. At Halloween, put up a mannequin wearing a scary mask or costume. Use holiday themes as a source for decorating ideas. For the rest of the year, try interesting eye catchers.

One of my roommates came up with an excellent eye catcher. While working for Nabisco he *liberated* "Mr. Oreo Cookie Man." Our friend, Mr. Oreo Cookie Man, was a large, inflatable Oreo cookie with hands, feet, and a smiley face. He sat in our window for an entire year, waving at pretty girls who passed our room.

The hallway walls and the outside of your door are also ripe for decorating. Get there before others do, and you will have large spaces for showing off your imagination and creativity to the rest of the dorm, if not to the whole wide world.

While dealing with unusual spaces and materials is fun, it is also time-consuming, so don't forget the simpler decorating items: wall posters, family photos, flags, and aluminum can sculptures.

CHAPTER 1: THE DORMITORY

One semester my roommates and I decided to construct a large collage in the hallway outside our room. Since our room was the last door on the floor, we reasoned that we owned the wall space of the entire back corner of the floor. We grabbed pictures from magazines, newspapers, and pamphlets and pasted them up creatively, in some cases making bold statements about life. Every scrap of paper with an image on it was fair game. We became the talk of the dorm. The girls living next door were inspired to make their own contributions to our collage.

BUNKING VERSUS LOFT BUILDING

The best way to expand the room's usable space is to attack the largest item(s) in the room. If the room is a double, you can bunk the beds. Even in a triple, you can bunk at least two of the beds. Most college beds are singles with interlocking frames, which allow you to stack them and to gain floor space. But before you commit to bunking, decide who will bunk on top. I suggest putting the shortest person on the bottom. This avoids a vertically challenged person having to step on the bottom bed in order to climb into the top bunk. Also, when a short person jumps down from the upper bunk, the inevitable "thunk" can wake you up at night.

A friend of mine would always warn me: "Don't take the top bunk. You could fall off and hurt yourself in a drunken stupor. It is a pain to get down quietly without waking up your bunkmate. Your bed will only be used for sleeping." On the other hand, if you own the bottom bunk, everybody will congregate on your bed and it will get dirtier."

During my junior year I learned the real downside of bunk beds. Here is one bunk bed story I am sure my former roommate would rather I didn't repeat. One night my *promiscuous* roommate felt inclined to bring home a girl. He and his lady crawled into the top bunk while I was sleeping in the bed below. Lets just say I woke

up to what I initially thought was an earthquake! Fortunately, the earthquake was merely the consummation of my roommate and his lady's new friendship. What is the moral of this story? I'll let you ponder that one.

Lofts are free-standing, space-saving structures that elevate a bed so that a desk can fit comfortably underneath. It places the bed at approximately the same height as the top of a bunk bed. Such an arrangement will let you save space, but you may not be able to stand at your desk, nor, if you're really tall, sit up in your bed. And you might bump your head on the ceiling when you climb out of bed.

Some lofts are very elaborate while others are nothing more than flimsy frames that hold up the bed. You can build one yourself or buy one from an upperclassman. If you buy a new loft, make sure you get directions on how to assemble it and a picture of how it should look once assembled. Also note that some dormitories are picky about furniture arrangements. So before you buy or build a loft, always check the housing guidelines you got from the college to make sure you are allowed to put one up.

LIGHTS

Dorm rooms are notoriously dark. In fact, dungeon-like is not too harsh a term. Bring a desk lamp from home, or get one before classes start. The best types are those that clamp onto the desk and swivel. With a swivel lamp you can direct light into different areas of the room. A dorm room can never have too much light. Bring extra light bulbs. That way you won't have to track down your resident adviser (RA) to get a new bulb when one goes bad at midnight before finals.

ADDITIONAL ROOM ENHANCEMENTS

MILK CRATES

Marilyn Monroe sang that diamonds are a girl's best friend, but milk crates are definitely a college student's best friend. They are strong and versatile. You can use them to pack your belongings when you are going to or leaving college. And during the academic year you can use them as storage cubicles. There's no such thing as too many milk crates. They also make great shelving, tables, CD holders, filing cabinets, and shower buckets.

A certain acquaintance of mine considered milk crates so valuable that he actually raided a supermarket and grabbed as many as he felt he needed. CAUTION: I do NOT recommend this course of action because it is quite illegal. It does emphasize, however, just how valuable these crates are to college students.

CARPETING

Your dorm room floor may need a little enhancing as well. A carpet or rug tends to make the room more attractive than the bare linoleum or wooden floors of most dorm rooms. And in colder climates floor coverings also keep your feet warm. Don't pay a lot. Don't buy the best: (1) because you are not likely not to have ample cash and (2) even if you're loaded with dollars, carpeting will get stained, dirty, and foul-smelling by the end of

the academic year. Buy remnants from carpet, discount, or department stores, or find "experienced" rugs at yard sales. If all else fails, you might hunt down an upperclassman, who is selling carpeting in reasonable condition.

PETS

Since you'll be living away from home it's natural to miss your pets, but most dormitories do not allow pets (other than fish or gerbil-sized animals). Bringing your dog or cat to college, therefore, is not wise and may well be impossible.

A bigger animal, such as a cat or a dog, can cause all kinds of problems in the confined space of a dorm room. First, the smell might be considerable and may be unbearable to at least some of your dormmates. Second, in college you usually won't have time to deflea or groom your pet or to take it to the vet. Besides, vets are not cheap, and you usually don't have much cash as a student. Third, animals often suffer all kinds of abuse from other students.

Here are some great examples as to why pets in a dorm are a bad idea!

During my freshman year, my RA decided to buy a small tropical bird. The little feathered animal chirped all night long. Once, when the RA went out for a night on the town, some pranksters broke into his room, removed the bird from its cage, and placed a cat inside. To make the situation more interesting, they stuffed the cat's mouth with bird feathers. The RA nearly lost his supper when he came home.

One of my roommates was probably the ultimate example of *why not to have a pet*. My roommate took great sadistic pleasure torturing a poor defenseless gerbil. My roommate had been snacking on a fried pizza roll and decided to share it with his gerbil. After each bite into the pizza roll, my roommate let the gerbil crawl inside the roll for a nibble. Once the two of them were finished with the pizza roll, my roommate used the gerbil as a hackey sack, tossing the poor critter into the air and letting it fall onto a beanbag chair. This went on until the sun came up. Needless to say, the gerbil did not live through summer break.

Lastly, during my senior year I lived in an apartment for one semester, where one of my roommates had a ferret. He rarely filled his pet's water bottle, so the poor thing often got a drink only when it tipped over a cup of vodka. It was intoxicated half the time.

THE RESIDENT ADVISOR (RA)

Living in a dorm room is like living in a community there are neighbors to contend with. Problems and disputes will occur. Count on it. And when things get messy, there has to be some sort of authority to straighten things out. Enter the RA, trained in counseling, safety, and the rules. The RA makes sure that none of the dorm inhabitants trash the place. If you have a roommate problem or a dispute with a neighbor, need a ride to the emergency room, or find a rat under the bed, you call the RA. Most RAs have open-door policies. They are there to help you solve any problem–from replacing light bulbs and fixing circuit breakers to arranging for emergency medical attention.

I have one friend who has exceptionally warm and positive memories of her freshman RA: "My RA was like a mother to me. A lot of girls didn't like her because she was old-fashioned. We hugged each other often. At the beginning of my first semester, when it was very lonely for me, she was always there with an open ear. I used to go to her with all my problems. She proofread my papers and gave me advice on disputes with friends."

IDENTIFICATION (ID) CARDS

Most dorms have security systems, including ID cards. These cards don't vary much from campus to campus. The size of a credit card and laminated, they contain your photo, student number, vital statistics, and usually a magnetic strip and/or bar code so they can be read by magnetic card readers and bar code scanners. You need this to gain entrance to your dormitory. It also keeps track of your meal purchases in the cafeteria and dining hall. Teachers' assistants (TAs) use ID cards to verify who you are when you take exams. This ensures that the name on top of the exam paper is the same as the person actually taking the exam. You usually need to show your student ID card to get student discounts both on and off campus. And sometimes mail order houses even require photocopies of the card when you make purchases from them. I recommend that you put this card on a string or chain to make it a necklace so you don't lose it; replacing this card is expensive.

TYPES OF DORM INHABITANTS

No discussion of dormitories would be complete without a rundown of the five basic characters that are guaranteed to inhabit every dorm. Some of these people are benign while others are nothing but a serious nuisance.

STEREO BLASTER

Some jerk always has to prove that he or she has the ultimate stereo, amplifier, and speakers. This person will blast his or her stereo system at the most inappropriate moments. Often this person feels that 3:30 a.m., or the night before a major exam is the best time to listen to a song at 100 decibels. There is a special section of hell reserved for this type of person.

PHANTOM

Don't ask me why, but there will always be a person living in your dorm about whom nobody will know a thing. This person will keep to himself or herself. You'll never know where this person is going or what he or she is up to. The phantom is seemingly benign, but one never knows.

ROMEO

Usually every floor has one of these. Typically this person is a guy with one hot and steamy love affair after another. His poor roommate not only ends up paying for a double occupancy room with triple occupancy, but will often spend nights outside the room so Romeo can spend quality time with his flavor of the week.

JERK

Basically this person represents all of the qualities that we don't admire in people: loud, obnoxious, and rude. This would be the person who starts his weekend on Wednesday and drinks until Sunday. This same person breaks and smashes things when he gets drunk. Pity the fool who is his roommate!

We had a stereo blaster in my dorm. This dodo would play his music so loud that his door would pulse with the rhythm! He would crank up his music so he could hear it in the shower! We nicknamed our stereo blaster "Woofer." My belief is that he went deaf after graduation.

During my senior year we had a phantom on our floor. He never spoke. In fact not one person who lived on my floor had ever heard his voice!

Four doors down from my room during freshman year lived a bona fide Romeo. This fellow had a hot and steamy love affair going 24 hours a day. His poor roommate spent more than a few evenings sleeping in the hallway.

I have known more than my share of jerks. My favorite jerk once barricaded the door to my room. He had me and a friend trapped. Our only escape was the window and a rope. The two of us had to descend three stories to reach safety!

THE PRANKSTER

I have reserved an entire section for this colorful individual! See chapter 11.

THE HOUSING AUTHORITY

Your dormitory is under the jurisdiction of the Campus Housing Authority or Campus Housing Office. The members of this team report to the Dean of Student Housing. In my view, there is very little difference between a typical college housing authority and a typical slumlord.

When you need to get immediate action, the housing authority, like the slumlord, drags its feet. I can remember once waiting an entire day to take a shower. Our dorm ran out of cold water. All our faucets and showerheads dripped scolding water. I nearly got burned. My roommates and I waited hours for the plumber to arrive.

Like a slumlord, the housing authority presides only over prime housing stock. To illustrate the high quality of dorm construction, consider what happened when somebody flushed a toilet in one of the dorms that I have inhabited. All the cold water in the showers would cut off while the toilet tank refilled, and the person taking a shower would get a hot flash!

I often felt that the builders of the RMS Titanic couldn't have done worse than the construction firm that put together our dorms. As the old saying goes: "Sure you'll have climate control. You'll have heat in the summer and air conditioning in the winter." In addition to the poor climate control, we also enjoyed closets that wouldn't close, and carpeting that had gone out of style in 1952 and hadn't come back in style by the turn of the millennium.

Just like the superintendent of a run-down apartment complex, the Dean of Housing provided little relief when things needed fixing. Whenever I approached him with a problem he seemed to have six excuses why he could not take action. Whatever happened to "The customer is always right?"

MY DORM SUCKS THE TOILETS LEAK. THE SHOWERS HAVE RUSTY WATER WON'T CLOSE AND THE HEATER DOESN'T WORK.

LET ME GUESS. YOU FOUND THE CHEAPEST CONTRACTOR AND MATERIALS TO BUILD THAT DORM

THATS NOT TRUE! WE USED THE SECOND CHEAPEST CONTRACTOR!

CHAPTER 2
WHAT TO BRING

College, unlike home, will not provide you with the creature comforts to which you are accustomed. You will need to take everything necessary for leading a functional life. I learned this lesson the hard way, during my first semester, because I had not taken many essentials. For your convenience and to keep you from going through the same trauma, I include a checklist in Appendix A that you can use to make sure you cover all the bases. As you pack for college, just check things off.

BEDDING, LINENS, AND TOWELS

THE BED

Let's start with basics. Obviously, you plan to sleep, right? Well, guess what? Your college bed may be nothing more than a cot with a single mattress. Even if it is a cut above minimum functional requirements, it certainly won't meet with Mom's approval. The mattress will probably have seen more than its fair share of action. Stains, spills, mildew, and other unspeakable residue may be present. Just anticipate such horror and pack a mattress cover. Slip it over the mattress before you put on the sheets. Make sure you fasten the cover with safety pins, because mattress covers have been known to pop off, usually in the middle of the night.

If you have any doubts about your mattress's past adventures, let me tell you about Boy Blunder. (After you have read this, you'll know why we called him Boy Blunder). He decided that the first decent snowfall of the year was too good to waste. Everybody was outside sledding downhill on lunch trays. But Boy Blunder had a better idea. He stripped his mattress bare, took it to the top of the highest hill, and enjoyed his padded ride all the way to the bottom, where he came to a stop in a patch of mud so that his entire mattress got covered with it. That's not all–Boy Blunder also discovered that, in the summer, his mattress made a great lawn chair. At the end of the freshman year, his mattress' bottom sported an attractive pattern of hardened mud and grass stains.

LINENS

Unlike in hotels, the military, or at home, sheets are not provided at college. Unless you plan on using a linen service, you need to bring at least two sets–a fitted bottom

and a flat top sheet, and a pillowcase. If you are a two-pillow sleeper, pack two pillowcases. Most college beds are either oversized or regular twins. Consult the housing literature the college sent you to determine the proper size. Be sure to bring blankets, but don't bother with a bedspread or comforter, because they will just get ruined or tossed on the floor.

TOWELS

And, of course, you'll need towels. Bring at least three sets. Try to rotate the sets so that you're always using reasonably clean ones.

If you don't want to truck in linens and towels, a linen service can supply both. Often these services are run by local laundromats. You pay a flat fee, and every week or so the service gives you clean towels, sheets, and pillow case(s).

My experience with such services is mixed. The towels and sheets were of institutional quality (hospital, hotel) and often stained. I was particularly distressed to find bloodstains on some of the towels. I advise against linen services.

Many colleges now sell you packages of towels and sheets. The main advantage is convenience. It is one less thing to bring with you, and the sheets are guaranteed to fit the bed. Remember, after four years of college both the sheets and the towels will probably have seen enough abuse to be discarded anyway.

PERSONAL HYGIENE

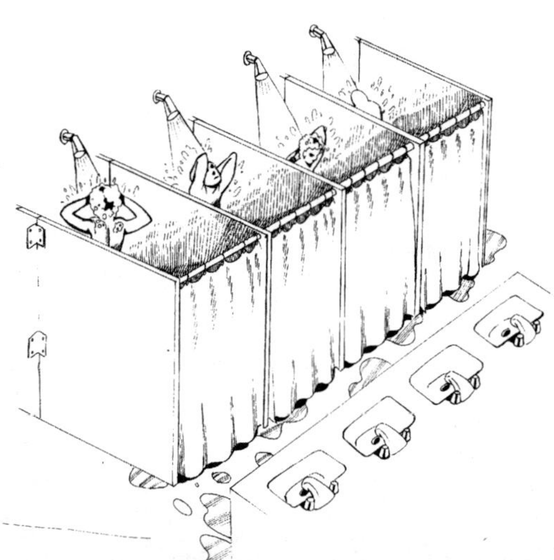

After the long drive to school, I'll bet you'll want a nice hot bath. Sorry, no can do. Most dorms don't have bathtubs. If you are a male freshman, most likely you will be using community showers. Remember high school gym class? There'll probably be four other people showering next to you. Some dorm showers have metal partitions with curtains that allow you some privacy while you strip before stepping into the shower. Women showers may offer a tad more luxury, but still the stalls may not have doors or curtains.

One college coed told me: "Two shower stalls for twenty girls! Fortunately there was both a door and a separator. I was grossed out by the showers at first. But then I got used to it. There was hair everywhere! The hair was by far the worst part of the experience."

Because there is a good chance that your showers will be down the hall in a community bathroom, there are a few items that you will want to take with you. The first item, **a bathrobe**, performs the vital function of covering you up *en route* to and from the bathroom. The second item, a **shower bucket or bag**, holds all your bathing needs, including soap in a plastic soap box, a face cloth, shampoo, hair conditioner, hair gel, body wash, and so on. Last but not least, you will want a pair of **tong sandals**. Why? Every day twenty or more students use this same bathroom. So you need to protect your feet from any stray foot fungi. The floor will, in fact, be loaded with all kinds of germs and such other goodies as the after-party vomit of binge drinkers.

In addition to shower needs, don't forget to bring other items for personal hygiene:

- ❑ Hairbrush, comb, barrettes, rubber bands, hair bow
- ❑ Hair dryer, curling iron
- ❑ Styling gel, mousse, hairspray
- ❑ Deodorant, cologne/perfume
- ❑ Toothbrush, toothpaste
- ❑ Dental floss, mouthwash
- ❑ Nail file and/or emery boards
- ❑ Clippers (finger- and toenails), tweezers
- ❑ Nail brush, cuticle remover, nail polish and remover
- ❑ Moisturizers and body creams
- ❑ Makeup (cosmetics, makeup remover, skin lotion, etc.)
- ❑ Razor and razor blades
- ❑ Shaving cream, styptic pencil, aftershave

I did a lot of research while I was in college, trying to find the best shave, one that was as close as possible without irritating my skin, I now pass the results on to freshmen males everywhere:
Electric razors versus razor blades—Electric razors never give as close a shave as blades do. I found, however, that the best way to get a close shave with an electric razor, is to use talcum powder sticks or Williams Lectric Shave, the latter being a pre-shave lotion that makes the hairs stand up so you can cut them more easily.

Shaving creams—Of all the creams I've tried, I prefer Edge Gel products, because they offer a variety of gels for different types of beards. This company's tough beard variety works best for me.

Razors—Gillette® MACH III gives a very close shave and is easy on the skin. I highly recommend it. I've tried every variety of disposable razors and blades. Some combinations, even though they give you a very close shave, often cause skin irritations and cuts. The MACH III gives a consistently smooth shave with no skin irritation.

Clothing

The type of clothing you'll need depends on the geographic location of your college. Obviously, in a warm climate, you'll need less and lighter clothing than if you have to dress for different and severely changing seasons.

The weather at my college was frigid six months of the year. (I once experienced –40 F!) Warm clothes were the secret to avoiding frostbite. I needed to wear a long heavy wool coat that wrapped around my entire body. My roommate, who had a crew cut, had to wear earmuffs to prevent frostbite! In fact, it often got so cold that I had to wear a scarf around my face to keep my nose hairs from freezing!

Undergarments

No matter what your climate, before arriving on campus pack as many undergarments (T-shirts, bras, panties, boxer shorts, briefs, and so on) and socks as possible. Ideally you should have enough socks to do laundry only once every couple of weeks. As a friend reminded me, "Bring more socks! You end up thinking you're going to do laundry, but never get around to it."

Daily Apparel

Always bring low-maintenance clothing, stuff that requires little or no ironing and can be worn more than once before it has to go to the laundry. You probably won't have the time to do ironing either. Sweatshirts and jeans are appropriate dress in college, especially in cooler climates. T-shirts and shorts are perfect for warmer regions. Of course, don't forget to bring comfortable walking shoes that are appropriate for your climate—work boots for cold and hostile environments, sandals and sneakers for more benign ones.

Dress Clothes

The issue of dress clothes is a trickier topic. Students at an urban campus tend to dress up more often to go clubbing (hanging out in the town's various nightclubs). Therefore, if you're living on an urban campus you'll probably need at least one set of dress clothes. Rural campuses tend to be more casual. If your campus is out in the boonies, bring only enough dress clothes for those rare occasions when you have a job interview or attend a gala event. You might even leave the dress clothes at home all together, if your parents live nearby.

The Unexpected

Of course, you can never anticipate your clothing needs entirely until you have actually arrived on campus. In a pinch, you're probably better off bringing too much than too

little. It's always far easier not to wear excess clothing than it is to get dressed in stuff you left at home.

Military surplus stores sell all kinds of used and new military clothing and equipment. These items are not only quite reasonably priced but durable, too. Surplus is a great way to pick up clothing without breaking your piggy bank.
One company you might consider contacting is:
I Goldberg International Surplus
902 Chestnut St.
Philadelphia, PA
(215) 925-9393
(215) 925-2955

ET CETERA

Finally, don't forget miscellaneous stuff. For cold climates, bring plenty of gloves. You'll want such items as a belt, baseball cap, backpack, and umbrella, regardless of the climate. If you wear glasses or contact lenses, bring a spare pair and the materials for cleaning and maintenance. In fact, bring a copy of your prescription, too. Last, but not least, don't forget your watch and wallet!

PHONES

While some campuses require that you bring or provide your own phone, others supply the phones. Some colleges may provide voice mail service. If your college doesn't offer such services and your roommate bungles messages, or if you live in a single room, you may want to get an answering machine to catch important calls.

Be sure to contact the campus housing authority to find out if a telephone or answering machine is necessary. Also ask about the arrangements for phone service.

One student gives this advice to those sharing phone service: "If you have to sign up for phone service with the local area phone company, make sure the phone is not taken out in your name. If so, you'll have difficulty collecting the last bill because it will arrive after everybody has left. There is usually a hookup fee or installation charge that you can get spread out over a few months. That way you don't have to pay for it all at once."

LONG DISTANCE SERVICE

Although your campus may provide a long distance service plan with a personalized PIN, look into the alternatives. You can't trust the campus housing authority to provide you the best long distance deal in town. Calling cards are one such alternative. These cards allow you to prepay for a fixed amount of long distance service. Another alternative is to get a cellular phone with a national long distance plan. Finally, you can use a web-based telephone. These web phones, which transfer your call across the Internet, are cheap, too, but the audio quality is often very poor.

CELLULAR PHONES

A cellular phone is always a good second phone to have. It allows people to reach you even when you are outside, and it comes in very handy in emergencies. Shop around for the best service plan that suits your needs. Look for the lowest monthly fee with the largest number of free air minutes.

BOOKS

Bring a dictionary and thesaurus. You'll need them when you write papers. See chapter 7 for more information on books.

LIGHTS

If you own a favorite reading lamp and if it's not too big (remember that space is always at a premium) bring it along.

ALARM CLOCK AND SLEEPING AIDS

Mom won't be around to wake you up for class, and you can't depend on a roommate to do it, so come prepared to have the job done mechanically by whatever device(s) necessary. Remember, if you oversleep and miss an exam, it might get a you a zero. It pays not to miss class because sometimes important course material is given only once. Simply put, you'll need at least one alarm clock. I advise you to place it across the room so you have to get up to shut it off. Otherwise there is too much temptation to hit the snooze bar. If you are particularly resistant to getting up on time, you might consider a couple of clocks set five minutes apart in separate parts of the room–if your roommate doesn't mind, of course.

Now for the other problem. It is always hard to go to sleep and stay asleep in a noisy freshman (and often upper-class) dorm. I found that earplugs are a must–to the point of often being the college student's best friend. They will filter out loud stereos, snoring, and the parties in the dorm that you don't attend for whatever reason. Just make sure they don't prevent you from hearing fire alarms and your alarm clock.

I offer this cogent comment about earplugs: "My roommate once snored so loudly that I had to go buy a pair. I got 29-decibel plugs, but discovered that they weren't effective enough. I had to leave the room, close the door, and sleep in the common area on a couch...and I could still hear my roommate! My advice is, always buy maximum strength ear plugs!"

CARPETING AND MILK CRATES

See the full discussion of these in chapter 1.

WASTEBASKET

Most rooms do not come with a wastebasket. Unless you want trash to pile up on the floor, get one. In addition, many colleges participate in recycling programs, so you may be required to separate your trash. In this case, you'll need more than one wastebasket.

TRUNK

If you live with an untrustworthy roommate or feel you need extra security, a trunk with a padlock can be a lifesaver. Put all your valuables (such as checkbook and credit cards) in it. Never use a lock with a key, because such locks can be picked easily or you might lose the key. Always use a combination lock, and keep the combination (once you've memorized it, of course) in a safe place (at home, for instance).

A trunk can be used as furniture, too. During my freshman year, my roommate and I needed somewhere to put our TV, VCR, and popcorn maker. Fortunately, our trunks were both of the same height, width, and depth. We stood them up vertically, and, with only minor tinkering, pulled the closet door from its hinges and placed it on top of the trunks. We then put a piece of carpeting on top of that, and, voila—instant table.

STATIONERY SUPPLIES

College wouldn't be any fun without writing, but stationery supplies can be expensive. My own experience has been that office-supply superstores like Staples and Office Max are the least expensive.

It's important to know where to find the best prices for these supplies as you will need:

- **Pens**—Bring as many as you can carry. People are always borrowing them but never returning them.
- **Pencils**—These are crucial, especially if you have math, economics, or science classes. Always buy pencils with (no. 2) lead, as all bubble-sheet exams require them. Also get a small pencil sharpener. Mechanical pencils are good, but they often run out of lead at the worst possible moment.
- **Eraser**—Bring a large one. Those itty-bitty ones on both mechanical and wooden pencils run out, especially during long, intensive exams in chemistry, physics, and calculus.
- **Post It Notes**—So you can leave messages to both yourself and roommates. They are also useful as bookmarks.
- **Blank Paper**—This is useful for homework, term papers, scratch paper, and so on. It might even do for the occasional letter to the folks. You know the one: "Dear Mom and Dad, I am fine.

- **Scotch Tape** – This stuff comes in handy all the time, for example, when your roommate accidentally steps on your completed homework and rips it.
- **Ruler** – Make sure it has both metric and standard (inch) measurements.
- **Mounting Putty** – A putty-like substance, available under the brand name Fun Tack, is perfect for putting up posters. Unlike tape, when you remove Fun Tack from a poster or the wall, it comes off.
- **Thumb Tacks** or **Drawing Pins** – Many dorm rooms have corkboards, and you might want to tack up a note on a public bulletin board.
- **Paper Clips**
- **Staples** and a **Stapler**
- **Glue Stick**
- **Calendar** (wall) and **Pocket Planner**
- **Calculator**
- **Note Books** (See Discussion in chapter 4.)

Health Supplies

A first-aid kit is vital. Minor scrapes and cuts can turn into major infections if you don't have bandages and antiseptic. Be sure your first aid kit contains:

- Bandages
- Antiseptic cream or ointment
- Surgical tape and scissors
- Antacid
- Pepto Bismol
- Aspirin or acetaminophen (such as Tylenol®)
- Any prescription medications you're taking
- Foot powder
- Vitamins
- Cough syrup
- Sunblock (if you're in a warm climate)
- Lipbalm (if you're in a cold climate)
- Facial tissues
- Cotton balls
- Retainers and mouth guard (if you grind your teeth or snore)
- Skin lotion
- Contraceptives
- Q-Tips
- Wash N' Drys

Laundry Supplies

Sooner or later you'll have to do laundry–it's inevitable! Unless, of course, you're the type who stockpiles laundry and takes it back to Mom as a homecoming present. Those of you who don't have that option will need:

- Laundry detergent
- Laundry bags (preferably one each for colored and white clothing)
- Laundry basket
- Ironing board (mini) and iron (if you must have clothes that need ironing)
- Antistatic sheets (to remove lint and static from clothes in the drying process)
- Lint remover (to get out stubborn lint)

MAJOR APPLIANCES

REFRIGERATORS AND MICROWAVE OVENS

Two appliances I consider indispensable are a microwave oven and a refrigerator. A microwave opens up a whole new world of quick meals and, most importantly, the production of large quantities of quick popcorn. And if Mom leaves you with a stash of home-cooked goodies, you'll need something in which to heat them.

A refrigerator is handy for very obvious reasons. It keeps soda cold, allows you to make your own ice cubes, and gives you a place to put perishable food. It can be the most costly appliance you own. Many schools now offer refrigerators for rent. In the short term, this is the cheapest solution, but, in the course of four years, it's probably better to buy your own, because you will have paid three times the value of the unit. If your roommate brings one, of course, you are all set. If it's up to you, I recommend buying one with a decent-size freezer compartment.

Some schools now offer refrigerator and microwave combination units for rent. These save space and are convenient. Again, it's probably cheaper in the long run to buy the individual appliances. Also if these items outlive their usefulness at the end of your senior year, you may be able to resell them to a freshman.

Don't forget to put baking soda in both the refrigerator and the freezer compartments to soak up odors. Buy dairy products in small quantities, because they spoil quickly. For example, if there is a power failure during the night, don't be surprised to find the milk you put in next morning's coffee to be a little sour!

TVS, DVDS, VCRS, AND STEREOS

Life in a dorm is always hard, and sometimes you just need to "vedge out." There's nothing more relaxing than popping a copy of The Matrix into your DVD player and cranking up the surround sound. It is probably one of the best stress relievers!

If you want to make new friends fast, just let the word spread that you'll be watching the latest action flick on DVD in your room on a Saturday night. Before you know it people will be pounding on your door. Of course, the downside is that people might also want to hang out in your room to watch "Friends," "X Files," or "Drew Carrey." Getting these people to leave could end up being a royal pain. I've lost sleep many times simply because I couldn't get fanatical television watchers out of my room.

If you decide to have a DVD player, I recommend getting one that plays DVDs, VCDs (video CDs), and CDs. A machine that plays all three saves you space. Some DVD players will also play MP3s!

If you keep a DVD player or VCR, here are the prerequisite college movies that no good dorm room should be without: Animal House, Revenge Of The Nerds, Road Trip, The Star Wars Trilogy, Lord Of The Rings, Montey Python and the Holy Grail, and The Matrix.

If you keep a stereo, don't forget headphones. There may be times when you want to listen to music but your roommate doesn't.

MISCELLANEOUS STUFF

SERIOUS AND USEFUL

Don't forget to bring hangers and closet organizers. Because dorm space is always at a premium, every inch counts. Use space as economically as possible to extend it. If you have a single bed (this won't work for lofts or bunk beds), get under-the-bed storage boxes. They are perfect for storing off-season clothes.

Don't forget such items as:

- ❑ Small sewing kit
- ❑ Tool box (hammer, screw driver kit, tape measure, etc.)
- ❑ Fan, space heater
- ❑ Paper towels (for emergency clean-up when your roommate drinks too much and gets sick–you don't want to muck up your good towels mopping it up!)
- ❑ Paper plates (for when the sub you ordered starts coming apart all over your desk or bed blanket)
- ❑ Air freshener
- ❑ Compact disk holder/CD wallet
- ❑ Can opener
- ❑ Bottle opener

FUN ITEMS

As the saying goes, "all work and no play makes Jack (or, to be politically correct, Jill) a dull person." Don't forget to bring things that will help break the stress and tension that comes from classwork, assignments, and exams. To ease tension and help maintain your balance, recreation is very important. Bring such things as:

- **Bat and Glove** — Perfect for getting an impromptu baseball or softball game going and a quick way to meet people.
- **Rollerblades** — An awesome way to get around. You haven't lived until you've skated inside the wonderfully smooth floors of the student union.
- **Playing Cards** — A low-tech way of having fun. You can play anything from solitaire to poker. Card games are great fun for both small and large groups of people.
- **Board Games** — Remember Monopoly, Battleship, or even Operation? Well, they are reborn in college.
- **Video Games** — Systems such as Sony Playstation, Ultra 64, and games like Game Boy and Game Gear. If you can't afford the latest and greatest video game system, an old Nintendo Entertainment System, or Sega Genesis will do. In fact old, 1980s' video game machines such as the Atari 2600, Mattel Intellevision, and ColecoVision are experiencing a revival. Units and their accompanying games can be picked up cheaply at thrift stores, yard sales, and flea markets.
- **Super Soaker** or **other efficient water delivery devices** — Every freshman goes through at least one water fight. Why be unprepared? Water fights relieve stress.

CHAPTER 3
SHOULD I BUY A COMPUTER?

Even the most jaded technophile often has difficulty purchasing the right computer. There are seemingly endless possibilities and the hardware changes every six months. To add further insult to injury, buying a computer is identical to buying a used car. You'll never be sure what is under the hood and the computer will have limited resale value.

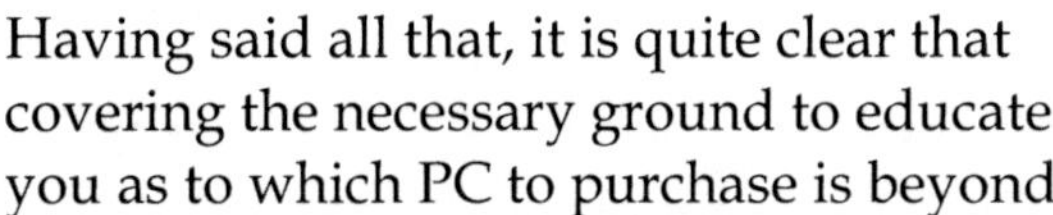

Having said all that, it is quite clear that covering the necessary ground to educate you as to which PC to purchase is beyond the scope of a single chapter in this book. I could easily fill pages with comparisons of such components as motherboards and graphics cards alone. Instead I will explain various peripherals, pieces of software, and Internet resources that might be of interest to a college student. Oh, and the answer is YES, YOU SHOULD BUY A COMPUTER!

PERIPHERALS

A computer without peripherals is essentially a box without a purpose. A device for linking your computer to the Internet is perhaps the most important of all the computer peripherals. Modems are a common way to get connected. The type of modem you need to purchase depends on the type of Internet connection that is available at your college. In fact some colleges bypass modems altogether and offer a direct campus network connection that requires a device called an Ethernet card. Consult with your campus housing authority to determine the sort of network capability and Internet availability in the dorms.

A flatbed scanner allows you to load pictures from Maxim or Cosmopolitan Magazine into your favorite graphics program. In order to document your college experience a digital camera is a must. You'll want to take many pictures so that when you are old and bald you can remember what you and your friends looked like at age 18. Digital cameras don't require film that needs to be developed. So you don't have to wait for days for prints to arrive. Once you've accumulated a stash of images you'll want to print them. An inkjet printer allows you to print your pictures as well as your assignments.

In my dorm we once had a student, we'll call him George, who antagonized his roommate to no end, but one day got his come-uppance. His roommate scanned both a picture of George and a picture from a men's magazine. He then made a composite of the two and made a ton of copies, which he put them up all over campus. The moral of the story: Digital technology is great!

An MP3 player can store all those music files that you downloaded off the Internet and lets you take them to class or the gym. Once you own an MP3 player you'll never go back to CD's. MP3s never skip and you don't have to worry about scratching them! The music is stored electronically.

Personal Digital Assistants, PDAs for short, are becoming almost as popular as cell phones. These gadgets let you keep track of appointments and exam dates, and allow you to play video games and music. They even let you retrieve Internet content. There are two major types of PDAs: Palm OS compatible and Microsoft Pocket PC compatible. The Palm variety is by far the most popular. It has the largest selection of software. However, the Pocket PC offers a richer multimedia experience and offers Pocket versions of Microsoft Office software (which includes such programs as Word and Excel).

PREREQUISITE SOFTWARE

I hate to sound like a shill for Microsoft, but—love'em or hate'em—this company's software is the standard. A copy of Microsoft Office is always a good idea. You will probably want to use MS WORD, PowerPoint, and Excel. These are the programs that you will encounter not just in the collegiate world but also in the business world later on. Familiarity with this software can only help you when it is time to get a job in the real world.

Here are some additional software packages you might wish to purchase:

Jasc Paint Shop Pro A great paint and image-editing program that is very powerful considering its extremely low price.

Corel Draw A fantastic drawing, paint, and image-editing package that provides excellent value for the money and can help you with countless projects. The images you create with Corel can be imported as graphics into such programs as Word and PowerPoint.

Net Objects Fusion This is the easiest-to-use and most powerful package for creating a professional-looking website

FAVORITE TECH-HEAD

There's always some dude on your campus who has the latest high tech toys. This is the person, who knows the hottest Internet sites and where to get the latest games. Get to know this expert and you'll be hooked up for life. Besides, your favorite tech-head is undoubtedly more useful than any tech support line you will ever call. A quick question to your new buddy and you might save yourself hours on the phone.

RESOURCES ON THE INTERNET

DIGITAL MUSIC

Digital music is the centerpiece of the college music experience. A few years ago students had to depend on such resources as radio and MTV to find the latest music, and getting copies of it often meant waiting in line at the local music store. Fortunately, the Internet has put music back into the hands of the music aficionados and out of the grubby paws of the evil record labels.

For almost 50 years the record labels took great pleasure in scalping music patrons with outrageous album prices and in using payola to dictate which music would be popular. Payola greased the palms of radio stations to get music airplay. The Internet, the great equalizer, allows bands that might not otherwise get exposure to get noticed. There are numerous websites where you can find bands that need a break and would really appreciate your attention. However, before I show you all the splendors of Internet music you'll need to become acquainted with some technology.

DIGITAL AUDIO FORMATS AND AUDIO PLAYERS

There are five major audio media formats that you ought to know about:

MP3 is an abbreviation for Motion Picture Experts Group Audio Layer 3. Music encoded in this audio format uses a type of compression that allows you to get near CD-quality audio within a fairly small file size. One of the more popular players for this audio format is a program called WinAmp. It is available at **www.winamp.com**.

WAVE, This is the audio format that is native to Microsoft Windows. Just about any audio player that runs on Microsoft Windows can play this format.

The next three audio formats handle what is called "streaming audio." With streaming audio, you can begin listening to the music before it has finished downloading off the Internet. The three most common streaming formats are:

Real Audio As of this writing. Real Audio is probably the most popular format for

streaming audio on the Internet. To listen to music in Real Audio Format, you need to download the Real Player, which is available at **www.real.com**.

Microsoft Media Player Microsoft has introduced its highly successful Windows Media Player as its own streaming audio solution. This program is also the native streaming audio format for the Microsoft Windows operating system. You can download it at **www.microsoft.com**.

QuickTime This is Apple's multimedia format for streaming audio and video. It can be downloaded at **www.quicktime.com**.

DIGITAL AUDIO TOOLS

Now that you are familiar with audio formats, there are a few tools that no digital audio buff should be without:

Cooledit This inexpensive program by Syntrillium Software packs quite a punch for very little money. It offers the ability to convert music from one audio format to another. It also lets you add special effects to audio, edit audio, perform mixes, and package audio for the Internet. It is also easy to use, because it features an intuitive user interface. You can download a trial version at **www.cooledit.com**.

Roxio Easy CD Creator This tool allows you to convert your CDs into MP3s and vice versa. It also allows you to turn scratched LPs into digital CDs. In terms of a price-performance ratio, this program, too, is very powerful. It is one of the most popular tools for burning both audio and data CDs. You can check them out at **www.roxio.com**.

Music Match This program is a digital music player and a whole lot more. It allows you to make your own CDs from MP3s. It also allows you to play MP3s, CDs, and Windows Media files. It is available at **www.musicmatch.com**.

INTERNET RADIO

Tired of listening to the same crappy music on mainstream radio stations? Does your campus radio station suck? Does your college town have only one radio station and it is an easy listening station? Thank goodness Internet radio has arrived with a vengeance.
Internet radio stations allow you to use streaming audio players to listen to broadcasts from the Internet. Unlike broadcast radio, Internet radio is not regulated by the FCC (at least not yet, as of this writing). These radio stations are often run by regular Joes, who, in a previous era, would have started pirate radio stations. Two of the more popular radio station sites are **www.shoutcast.com** and **www.live365.com**.

Most major radio stations also simulcast their programs on the Internet. If you want to listen to your hometown station while you are out of state, there is a good chance that you can access the station's website for a live audio feed.

For example, if you are from the Boston area, you might be interested in listening to **www.wbcn.com, www.wbz.com** , and **www.wrko.com**.

FINDING RADIO STATIONS

Just as with television, everybody has different viewing and listening habits. To find a station that caters to your particular tastes, check out these three websites:

The Radio Locator This site lists over 10,000 radio station web pages, 2500 audio streams. It is a radio search engine **www.radio-locator.com**.

Virtual Tuner This is a directory of over 10,000 TV and radio stations. It allows you to search for streaming media sources **www.virtualtuner.com**.

Microsoft Media Radio Tuner Microsoft maintains its own list of Internet radio sites that use the Microsoft Media Player audio format. **www.windowsmedia.com/radiotuner/**

PUTTING TOGETHER YOUR OWN RADIO STATION

If, after having searched the internet, you still cannot find what you like to listen to, consider setting up your own radio station. Besides, after the movie Pump Up The Volume, doesn't every guy secretly crave to have his own pirate radio station? Hey guys want to pickup chicks? Tell the gals that you've got your own pirate radio station and you can play their requests 24 hours a day. The best part of having an Internet pirate radio station is that the FCC won't try to shut you down.

Setting up a radio station is easier than you think. Both Shoutcast and Live365 let you do it at NO COST to you.

According to Shoutcast's website, "Shoutcast is a free-of-charge audio homesteading solution. It permits anyone on the Internet to broadcast audio from their PC to listeners across the Internet or any other IP-based network (Office LANs, college campuses, etc.)."

If you are really curious about putting up an Internet radio station, Ben Sawyer and Dave Greely wrote the book, "Online Broadcasting Power!" (ISBN: 096628898X). This book covers such topics as the basics of Internet radio, building a radio station on Shoutcast, and preparing content for your radio station.

FREE MUSIC

Is there really such a thing as a free lunch? On the Internet there is! Believe it or not, it is possible to get just about any piece of popular music for free. Special websites called file sharing networks allow you to obtain music for a download in MP3 format. Just search on such criteria as Artist or Song Name. This is definitely a gray area of the law. The most famous of these services is Napster. As of this writing, Napster has become a pay service.

THE TECHNOLOGY OF FREE MUSIC

File sharing network services link PCs belonging to the service members into a network so that everybody can find audio files stored on another member's PC. Subscribers simply agree to share audio files for free. This is known as "peer to peer." These file swapping sites let you swap music, video, and in some cases programs. Beside the legal issues, there are a few disadvantages to these services. First, what is on the network varies from minute to minute depending on who is logged in and which files they are sharing on their hard disk. Second, a person who is sharing the file you want could log out while you are downloading, and your copy might end up incomplete.

THE MOST POPULAR FILE SHARING NETWORKS

This information is provided for education use only. This author does not condone piracy of any sort! Before utilizing any of these websites, remember - you may be breaking the law. See the *ethics* lecture included in the upcoming paragraph. The reason I am revealing these dubious websites is to make you aware of what they are, and that they exist, as your peers will undoubtably acquaint you with them, if I don't. IF YOU DECIDE TO BREAK THE LAW - YOU DO SO BEING INFORMED OF THE RISKS.

www.aimster.com
www.bearshare.com
www.kazaa.com
www.limewire.com
www.audiogalaxy.com
www.musiccity.com

QUICK GUILT TRIP ETHICS LECTURE

Remember one thing, if you decide to use one of these services: When you download an audio file, the artist who created the music is not being paid. Artists depend on royalties from album sales and song play to earn a living. Granted, many music labels would be guilty of not sharing the spoils with their artists. The recording industry prosecutes those who download copyrighted music without permission. I urge you, if you find a piece of music that you like, please consider purchasing the music legitimately. This is especially crucial in the case of struggling artists from the local music scene. They need all the support they can

get. More importantly, sites such as **itunes.com** or **Napster.com** will allow you to purchase music legally. **Utilize the pay-per-download sites, or you may end up reading this book behind bars or end up paying hefty fines.**

WEB-BASED EMAIL

Most colleges offer a campus-based email solution. However, it is often necessary to have access to your email when you are away from school. Web-based email services such as **hotmail.com** and **yahoo.com** allow you to check your email from any computer in the world with a web browser. So if you are on spring break and walk into an Internet café in the Bahamas you can check your email from your girlfriend. Or during winter vacation you can keep in touch with your classmates via email without having to call them on the phone and pay long distance charges. Last but not least, web-based email systems give you a permanent address. So when you graduate from college you will still have your Hotmail or Yahoo accounts, whereas your campus account will almost certainly get deleted after graduation.

SEARCHING THE INTERNET

Search engines allow you to look up websites based on keywords that you enter. Even the best search engines do not cover the entire World Wide Web. Based on personal experience I'd say Google (**www.google.com**) has the most comprehensive coverage. It is one of the fastest engines and has the fewest ads.

Directories, unlike search engines, search for websites by categories. Typically the directory's homepage lists the searchable categories. One such directory is the Open Directory Project, **www.dmoz.com**.

BOOKING A TRIP HOME / SPRING BREAK

One of the greatest things about the Internet is the ease with which it lets you shop competitively for airline fairs and vacation deals. It is now possible to search for last-minute airline deals, vacation discounts, and cheap getaways. The following are the more popular travel websites on the Internet. So next time you need a flight home for the holidays or a cheap way to the Bahamas for spring break I recommend surfing the following sites:

Orbits.com This website is run by the airline industry. It allows you to check for flights by major airlines to and from just about any destination.

Expedia.com This website is owned by Microsoft and allows you to book vacation packages and flights. I have used it numerous times to book flights to Las Vegas and have consistently found good value for my money.

Priceline.com You've probably seen the obnoxious commercials for this site. It lets you to get last minute airline deals. However, until you have given your credit card number you won't know what you have just booked. If you don't feel comfortable buying a pig in a poke, you might want to stay away from this site.

KILLER WEBSITES YOU DEFINITELY WANT TO KNOW

MOVIES

What would college life be like without the occasional trip to the movies. With movie ticket prices escalating everyday you can no longer afford to go to the movies uninformed. Many of these sites let you get the scoop on movies before they even left the script writing phase!

Ain't It Cool News This website is the granddaddy of all movie news websites. The webmaster, Harry Knowles, is a self-proclaimed movie geek. His spies sneak onto movie sets, studio test screenings and, in some cases, get tours into the most secret places in the movie industry. The movie studios know that if Harry Knowles puts out the word that a movie is bad, there is a good chance it is going to tank at the box office. Some people may say that Steven Spielberg is the most influential person in Hollywood, but those of us who surf the net know it is Harry Knowles. **www.aint-it-cool-news.com**

Darkhorizons.com This is a very cool and extremely informative website run by Garth Franklin. Whatever may fall through the cracks at Ain't It Cool News is sure to be picked up by this site. Garth's site is meticulously well organized and updated almost every weekday with the juiciest movie news on the net.

TheForce.Net Psst! Want the latest Star Wars news? Do you want to know what is going on in the Star Wars prequels? Here is the site that spills the dirt before it hits the theatres.

PURCHASING MOVIE TICKETS

Why purchase tickets on-line? Well the bottom line is this. If you live in a major metropolitan area where lots of people go to the movies, there is a chance that your movie will sell out. It happens a lot especially on opening night of a major release. You pay for this convenience with a surcharge on each ticket, but it is better than showing up at the theatre and finding out that you can't get a ticket at all.

Here are two fairly popular movie tickets sites: **www.fandango.com** and **www.movietickets.com**.

NEWS

Even though you are in college you probably want to keep up with what's going on in the world, and there are many news sources on the Internet to choose from. I've listed

those that I think are among the better ones.

www.slashdot.org These guys are the ultimate geek news source. Their tagline says, "News For Nerds." No matter what, this site gets the dirt in the high tech world.

www.cnn.com This site is as good as its live cable television counterpart. You can also sign up for news alerts, in which case you will be emailed as things happen.

www.msnbc.com This is another great general news site that is as good as its cable counterpart.

www.news.com Here is a great source of high tech news. Want to know what is going on with the major high tech companies? Surf here and be enlightened.

REFERENCE

Do you need some information for an assignment? These sites contain all kinds of reference material to assist you.

Bablefish This site is a translation engine. It allows you to translate from foreign languages such as Italian, Spanish, German, Chinese, etc into English. The translations are not perfect but they'll help you get the basic idea of what is being expressed. The site lets you submit an entire web page for translation! **babelfish.altavista.com**

Thesaurus.com This site has a large database of synonyms. (Something the author should have consulted much more frequently while working on this book.)

YourDictionary.com This site contains links to various dictionaries and thesauruses.

Encylopedia.com This site lets you to search the Columbia Encyclopedia.

WEBSITES TARGETING COLLEGE STUDENTS

www.collegiatemall.com Need sheets, towels, appliances, or a bean bag? Don't have time to go shopping? Lack a car to take the stuff home. This site has just about everything a college student would need to furnish a dorm room, and then some. According to the company web site, "As a company largely consisting of students and recent graduates, we are very familiar with the college shopping experience… We have pooled our collective experience to create what we believe is the most convenient shopping alternative with the widest selection available."

www.student.com This is a web community for college students. Offers clubs, matchmaking services, and articles on topics of interest to college students.

www.collegeclub.com This web portal for college students is part of the Student

Advantage Network.

www.edu.com This site sells software, computers, peripherals, and electronics to college students at a discount.

www.studentrewards.com Need money for school? Need a scholarship? Here's a site you should browse!

www.campusfood.com This site features on-line menus for ordering at restaurants in the area around your college. According to this website there are over 1,000 restaurants and 200 schools across the country in the campusfood.com network. Ordering out has never been easier. I took this site for a test spin. One pizza restaurant allowed me to create my own custom pizza on-line and tallied up the order as I made it!

www.bolt.com The following is taken directly from this website: "Bolt is a leading Web and wireless platform for 15 to 24 year olds that provides cutting-edge communications tools that enable young adults to interact in a relevant, member-created environment. Whether on the Web or via wireless devices, Bolt members express themselves and speak their minds on whatever they want. From dating to current events, final exams to MP3s—the discussions on Bolt are driven by our members"

PUTTING UP YOUR OWN WEBSITE

Eventually you might want to consider having your own little spot on the Internet. Fortunately, there are a few services that will host your website at no cost. These services are for non-commercial websites.

www.geocities.com This is part of the Yahoo! Network. This service offers you 15 megabytes of free disk space on its server, page building tools, statistics on who is visiting your website, a file manager, and ftp access.

www.angelfire.com Angelfire is part of the Terra Lycos Network. It offers 20 megabytes of free disk space on its webserver, page building tools, and page design templates. It also offers over 10,000 pieces of clip art to use with your website!

CHAPTER 4

EATING AND DINING OPTIONS

I could easily fill an entire book on freshman eating habits. During my first year in college, I not only gained the traditional "freshman 15 pounds," but also earned my masters degree in caffeine and junk food. The two cavities I acquired in that one year were courtesy of my atrocious eating habits. Sugar alone is not a basic food group. Neither are JELL-O®, animal crackers, Kool-Aid®, or Fun Dip.

THE MEAL PLAN

The campus dining hall food cured me of any future desire to eat French fries, fried potatoes, home fries, or even hash browns. Bacon drenched in grease made my stomach do spin cycles. Powdered eggs, served every morning accompanied by butter-drenched toast, was my college's version of a student power breakfast.

But you do have to supply your body with some sort of nourishment, and Kellogg's Frosted Flakes will get you only so far. Eventually you must break down and eat a hot meal. Freshmen, unfortunately, have little or no choice in their food source. Most likely you'll end up on the campus meal plan and have to eat in the dining hall.

Most colleges offer two dining options. First there is the **Standard Meal Plan**. In this option you are issued a certain number of meals per day (usually totaling 7, 10, 14, or 19 meals per week). Meals are to be consumed at regular hours in a particular dining hall. Normally these meals are by the all-you-

can-eat rule, with the stipulation that you can't remove food from the cafeteria. You pay a flat fee for the meal instead of having to pay for each item on your plate. However, you must eat when they tell you to and select one of the entrées offered. Another thing to keep in mind is that many campuses serve only two meals on Saturdays and Sundays—brunch and dinner.

Then there is the **Declining Balance Plan**. You deposit a certain amount of money into a campus meal account. For each meal you eat, you deduct a certain number of dollars. Deductions are based on what you purchase—each item on your tray counts, including the packet of butter. This plan allows you to eat outside the cafeteria at such places as campus snack bars and pizzerias, but this can get extremely expensive, especially if you're are a big eater. On some campuses you can buy balance points for less than their face value from other students who have extras.

THE DINING HALL

Sometimes campus dining services offer specials. For example, at my college, on the standard meal plan, I got a good monotony breaker on Friday nights. The campus pizzeria offered what was known as "Happy Hour." No, there was no booze, but the student meal card gave me three slices of pizza and a medium soda. To make the deal sweeter, the pizzeria showed movies from 5:00 PM until 7:00 PM, the length of Happy Hour. Those were the days!

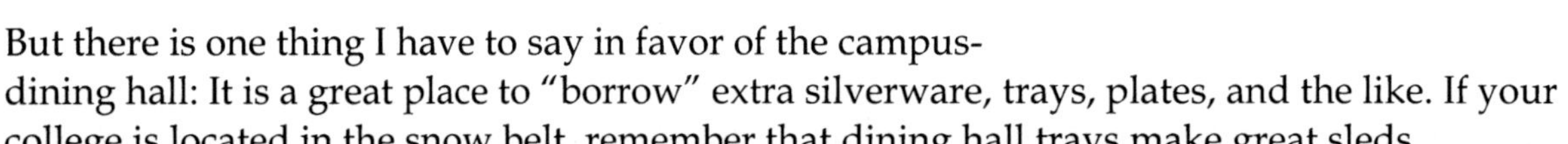

But there is one thing I have to say in favor of the campus-dining hall: It is a great place to "borrow" extra silverware, trays, plates, and the like. If your college is located in the snow belt, remember that dining hall trays make great sleds.

Dining halls definitely contribute their share of college horror stories. I've never met a student who had anything pleasant to say about college dining halls. The food is usually high in fat and low in taste. One student once told me: "When they [dining-hall managers] name the food, you'd better worry. Blackened Chicken means that they can do anything to it, even burn it, and it will always taste awful."

Another student almost ended up in the emergency room. "We had a general outbreak of food poisoning from the Chicken Alfredo," he reported.

Last but not least a health conscious patron of campus dining remarked: "Everything in the café has too much oil and grease. They fry everything there. Not good if you are concerned about your health!"

For me, campus dining often got monotonous. All entrées tasted like rubber and paste. There came a point when I couldn't look at another gristleburger or petrified hot dog. The solution, of course, was off-campus dining.

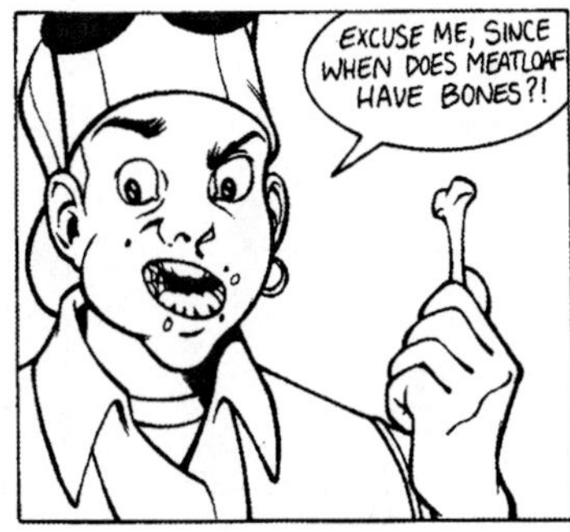

EATING OUT

Many restaurants in college towns offer deals for students. For example, in my college town, both Burger King and Ponderosa Steak House offered a 10-percent discount to students on a meal plan. My friends and I often feasted on the buffet at Ponderosa. We would starve all day and then eat like pigs in the evening. One restaurant offered a 14-inch pizza, choice of any sub, two Cokes, and a bag of chips for $5 and change. Now that's a deal! Check with your local restaurants for details on various deals and discounts. Remember, these places want your business and will resort to all kinds of tactics to get it.

Dining out can have its pitfalls. Right before an evening exam, for instance, I was usually too nervous to eat, but after the exam, I tended to get a delivery from the local Greek deli joint, which made a great sandwich called a "gyro." The sandwich was made of pita bread stuffed with spiced lamb, yogurt sauce, lettuce, and tomato. Needless to say, I ate a lot of them. A few days after being home for summer vacation I received a letter in the mail. The Board of Health had closed the deli because of a hepatitis outbreak. I had eaten there only a day or two before the outbreak! Fortunately, I didn't contract the illness, but I kept a key chain the owner had given me as a good luck charm anyway.

My personal favorite off-campus meal was a Sicilian-style sheet pizza, delivered. Sheet pizzas are over two feet long, two inches thick, and fairly wide. There are 24 slices, so one of them could feed six people easily. Such pizzas usually retail for around $20

with a plain-cheese topping. This comes out to only $3.33 per person. Prices, of course, will vary, but it's still a good deal. And if you are feeling greedy you can buy one, put it in the fridge, and live off it for several days. Recently, Taco Bell has been gaining in popularity on campuses because the food is cheap, soda refills are infinite, and three or so tacos can fill usually up an entire college student.

MICROWAVE FOOD

Sooner or later every college student becomes initiated into the wonderful world of microwaving. Whether you're looking for an alternative to campus dining or just trying to satisfy the midnight munchies, you'll eventually end up digging into the frozen food section of the local supermarket. Unfortunately, I've had the highly overrated pleasure of trying a good portion of these foods.

While combing through the frozen food aisles of my local college-town supermarket, I filled my shopping cart with nearly every imaginable product from the freezer. I learned the hard way, which items gave me indigestion or tasted terrible. Nearly every form of frozen pizza was bad for my stomach lining.

On the positive side, I found both Budget Gourmet and Healthy Choice meals to be quite edible. I have the following to report:

- **The Budget Gourmet** The Budget Gourmet Light series is low in both fat and calories and offers the best value for the money. A typical meal has around 250 calories and 6 grams of fat. Entrées include such tasty delights as Lasagna with Meat Sauce, Chinese-style Vegetables and Chicken, and Penne Pasta with Chunky Tomato Sauce and Italian Sausage. The only disadvantage is that the meals must be eaten directly from the box or poured onto a plate after being microwaved.
- **Healthy Choice**—These are higher-quality dinners that are also low in fat and calories. A typical meal has around 270 calories and 4 grams of fat. Entrees include such culinary works of art as Country Herb Chicken, Chicken Teriyaki, and Chicken Parmigiana. The

dinners come in a handy microwaveable plastic plate.

CANNED SOUP

Canned soup is one of those non-perishable items you can buy on sale and let sit on a shelf until needed. Though all canned soups look rather similar on the outside, they are clearly not created equal on the inside! They vary greatly in calories, fat, sodium, and serving size. Consider the following comparison of minestrone soups:

	Brand A	*Brand B*	*Brand C*
Serving Size	305 grams	245 grams	241 grams
Calories	140	120	110
Calories From Fat	30	25	10
Sodium	1,220 milligrams	510 milligrams	390 milligrams
Total Fat	3 grams	2.5 grams	1 gram

...or this comparison between two so-called healthy Chicken Noodle soups:

	Healthy Choice Old Fashioned Chicken Soup	*Progresso Healthy Classics Chicken Noodle Soup*
Serving Size	250 grams	237 grams
Calories	140	80
Calories From Fat	25	15
Sodium	400 milligrams	480 milligrams
Total Fat	3 grams	2 grams
Cholesterol	10 milligrams	20 milligrams
Total Carbohydrates	20 grams	10 grams
Protein	9 grams	7 grams

Although the Progresso has the smaller serving size, it's higher in sodium, and cholesterol. With a mere 13 additional grams in serving size, Healthy Choice has almost double the calories and carbohydrates. The bottom line is that you are damned it you do and damned if you don't. Eating healthy doesn't necessarily mean eating low-calorie food.

CANNED SPAGHETTI

Growing up in an Italian household, I had never been a fan of spaghetti in a can. However, many of my "taste-bud challenged" friends found the stuff irresistible. In fact I knew one guy who ate it directly from the can without heating it. Yuck! At my house my mother, the Italian chef, deemed canned spaghetti unfit for human consumption and fed it to the dog. (We had a very resilient dog at home!) If for some strange reason you find the stuff appealing, please consider the following comparison between two cans of spaghetti, one store-brand, the other the leading national brand:

Beef Ravioli In Tomato Sauce Comparison

	Store Brand	*National Brand*
Serving Size	240 grams	244 grams
Calories	200	230
Calories From Fat	30	45
Total Fat	3 grams	5 grams
Cholesterol	10 milligrams	20 milligrams
Sodium	1,430 milligrams	1,150 milligrams
Total Carbohydrates	36 grams	37 grams

Note that there isn't much of a difference between the two versions of canned spaghetti. They both come in nearly the same serving size, with roughly the same amount of fat and calories. Where they differ is in price! The leading national brand is nearly 25 percent more expensive. Often the leading national brand and the supermarket brand are manufactured on the same assembly line! In this particular case, the cans were identical in size and shape. The only discernible difference was the label...and guess which of the two labels was actually more attractive? What's the point? You can save money without sacrificing quality by sticking with supermarket brands.

COOKING

Of course, if microwave cuisine is not for you and if, at some point, you move into an apartment, you might want to try real cooking. Before you get any grand illusions about becoming a gourmet chef, let's get one thing straight cooking is a lot of work. Making the food is only half the work. You also have to clean up pots, pans, plates, and utensils.

One semester, I lived with six other guys in an apartment and was occasionally called on to be a short-order cook. Cooking for seven people requires lots of patience. Dinner is never ready soon enough. There is always some wise-ass who complains about the cuisine. This same person, of course, will never volunteer to cook!

Our menus were typical bachelor food (which stands for "cheap and easy to prepare"):

- ❑ **Macaroni And Cheese** We had this more often than I now care to remember!
- ❑ **Burritos** No, not the homemade variety, but the ones from the refrigerator section of the supermarket.
- ❑ **Taco Salad** The one time a week when I actually got to eat vegetables (what a concept!).
- ❑ **Fried Chicken Patties** Again, these were cheap and quick (especially because we had a deep fryer).
- ❑ **Pancakes** And you thought they were just for breakfast!
- ❑ **Stir-Fry** Whatever was left in the fridge went into this. A generous addition of maple syrup always made it taste better.
- ❑ **Pizza** Our budget included an allocation for a sheet of pizza every Friday night.

I confess that, over time, the meals deteriorated. As exam time crept up and assignments got more difficult, the menu became less elaborate. In fact, such amazing dishes as peanut butter and jelly sandwiches eventually became a nightly occurrence.

Finding out who among your roommates can cook is an exercise in trial and error. One of my roommates was a disaster waiting to happen. One day he decided to marinate steaks in an entire bottle of olive oil. For those of you unfamiliar with the properties of olive oil, it's a natural laxative. The steaks were so laden with oil that all of us had to hold our stomachs for the entire night. To make things worse, the oil that didn't go on the steaks ended up inside the oven. A week later when we were baking pizzas, gray smoke started pouring out of the oven. You guessed it, it was the olive oil, rock-hard and burnt to a crisp

Among the disadvantages of having a kitchen in our apartment were the insane cooking experiments that some of my roommates perpetrated:

The chocolate chip cookie dough hangover My roommates used to enjoy eating raw cookie dough, when they got drunk. So they once made a large batch of chocolate chip cookie dough in a punch bowl. They put it somewhere in the apartment and then promptly forgot it after the hangovers had subsided. Weeks later somebody discovered the bowl...and its unsavory green mold!

Microbrewing My roommates and I (all seniors) decided the best way to pick up girls was to invite them to a brewing party. Of course, in order to have the party we needed to brew beer (a minor technicality). We spent nights sterilizing bottles in a kettle over the stove. Then, of course, came the wonderful fermentation process (yes, there was the distinct odor of malt, yeast, hops in the air). Weeks later the beer was ready, but unfortunately, undrinkable. Not only did it taste like chemical waste, but no girls showed up for the party either, and we had one huge mess to clean up.

I soon learned that apartment living wasn't all it was cracked up to be. Keeping the kitchen up and running was a full-time job for one of our roommates. He became our official domestic "authority figure." He made sure everybody paid his fair share of the food bill. He also scheduled people for cooking and cleaning up. But the system never really worked: At least one of our roommates was always late in paying for the food. Nobody ever wanted to be the clean-up crew for the kitchen. And some people ate more than their

fair share while others went hungry.

To cook you need to plan your meals and portions, especially if you want to cook well. Cooking a meal for just one person is the hardest, and you'll often have food left over. If you want to cook while living away from home, first practice at home. Get to feel comfortable behind the stove. Then master a couple of never-fail recipes.

If you're clumsy (like me) or need inspiration before you hit the stove, consult a cookbook. Here are a few books that are worth consulting:

- **The College Cookbook : An Alternative to the Meal Plan by Geri Harrington [ISBN: 0882664972 , Storey Books]**
- **Cooking Without A Kitchen : The Coffee Maker Cookbook by , (Editor), (Editor), Th. Ricks [ISBN: 0963706217, MCB Publications]**
- **The Healthy College Cookbook : Quick, Cheap, Easy by Alexandra Nimetz, Jason Stanleu, and Emeline Starr [ISBN: 1580171265, Storey Books]**
- **The Kitchenless Cookbook by [ISBN: 096621370X, InterMedia Publishing, Inc.]**
- **Microwave Cooking for One by [ISBN: 1565546660, Firebird Press]**
- **The Starving Student's Cookbook by Dede Hall [ISBN: 0446395307, Warner Books]**
- **Tray Gourmet: Be Your Own Chef in the College Cafeteria by , (Contributor), (Illustrator) [ISBN: 0962740322, Lake Isle Press]**

Trying to cook without the benefit of a real kitchen tends to be a futile affair. While I was living in my single-occupancy dorm room, I once had a craving for chicken stir-fry. I searched for the next best thing to a stove and found a hot plate with a full-size burner, big enough to hold a pot. I plugged in the hot plate, the electric can opener, the microwave, and the TV. And wouldn't you know it, just as the chicken was starting to cook, out went all the lights. I had tripped the circuit breaker and had to wait for the RA to reset it before I could finish my cooking. Tripping the circuit breaker every time I heated anything on the damn hot plate cured me of all desire to keep on cooking.

Here is my personal favorite among my cooking stories: One day I heard the smoke detectors go off in the lavatory. I walked in and discovered two guys cooking meat with an electric frying pan. They had sautéed their meat in a bottle of cooking wine...and the meat was venison from a deer they had shot earlier in the week. But why did they have to prepare their food in the bathroom?

CHAPTER 5
SNACKING

Undoubtedly a major part of any college student's life is snacking. Staying up late, studying, and even partying will give you the munchies. I consider myself a connoisseur of sugar-laced energy boosters and of liquid caffeine. So I will now pass my snack knowledge on to you.

SODA AND OTHER BEVERAGES

Soda is expensive, especially if, like me, you are brand-name loyal. I enjoy a certain cola that comes in a red and white can that always produces a smile. During my college years, however, I found that economics outweighed brand-name loyalty. Most supermarkets offer their own brands of soda. This stuff goes for as little as 15 cents a can. Generic brand, three-liter bottles are quite a bargain for the money. No-name brands can be bought at wholesale discount stores like BJ's, Sam's, or Costco for exceptional savings.

Powdered beverages are another alternative. My college's drinking water, however, was so foul that even the best of the powdered drinks couldn't mask the taste of chlorine and other chemicals. As far as pure flavor goes, I've found Kool-Aid® to be the best. And it comes in such amazing varieties of flavors, such as Sharkleberrry Fin, that you'll never get bored. And, the more Kool-Aid® you buy, the more points you can earn toward free stuff such as their famous punch bowl. A friend of mine saved enough points to get the punch bowl AND a set of matching cups.

My final word on powdered drinks, though, is cautionary. Stay away from diet shakes like Ultra Slim Fast. Thinking I was smart, I drank the stuff to avoid one meal a day. It tasted great going down, but within an hour my stomach was doing spins, and I had major gas and bloating. The stuff is high in fiber and acts like a laxative.

If you are on a health kick, allow me to clear up a few fallacies. Pure fruit juice does not mean the same as low in calories. A juice box can have as many as 120 calories, only 20 calories less than a can of Coca-Cola, which has 140 calories. Ultimately the healthiest beverage to drink is bottled water. However, if you're calorie conscious and want something sweet to drink, diet soda is probably your best bet.

If you're going to drink bottled water, make sure it's from a real spring. Avoid distilled

water it's for ironing clothes, not hydrating people. The best bottled water I've discovered is flavored seltzer water. Poland Spring®, Polar, and Adirondack® make non-caloric seltzers that include such flavors as lemon, mandarin orange, and raspberry lime.

COOKIES

Again, this is a question of brand-name loyalty. I had a roommate who swore by Nabisco, especially its Snackwell's® line of low-fat temptations. I discovered, however, that supermarket brands were a lot cheaper and tasted pretty good, too. The only difference between my supermarket's animal crackers and one of the national brands were 50 cents of my scarce money supply. Nobody will ever think any less of you for eating Hydrox instead of Oreo cookies, and to my taste, Little Debbie snacks and pastries are cheaper and better than Hostess.

HEALTH FOOD

What can I say? You're in college, nobody expects you to eat healthy. That's why, once you have your first job you'll have to spend lots of money each month for a membership in a fitness club to lose the 20 or so pounds you put on in college. If you really feel like having a snack that's low in fat and calories, try rice cakes. Quaker puts out packages of mini rice cakes in such flavors as honey nut, caramel, and apple cinnamon. Each cake has only 10 calories. A full serving has only 50 calories, and the whole bag, only 100.

Another item is hot-air-popped popcorn. Unfortunately, I can't give you the exact number of calories per serving, but it's fairly low. Not only is popcorn a good source of dietary fiber, it's also easy to make. You don't even need a hot-air popper. Just take a handful of kernels, toss them into a paper lunch bag, and fold the top down so the bag is sealed. Then microwave the bag for about three minutes or until there are more than 10 seconds between the popping of individual kernels. Unfortunately, microwave popcorn that comes in a little packet, such as Pop Secret, is high in calories and loaded with such nasty things as partially hydrogenated cottonseed oil. Remember that cottonseeds come from cotton plants, which are grown and sprayed for clothes, not food! We won't even talk about most movie-theater popcorn.

The last healthy food you might want to try is tortilla chips and salsa. Tortilla chips are now available baked instead of fried. They not only taste good, they're also low in fat and calories. The best part is that salsa has no fat and is totally good for you.

MARSHMALLOW FLUFF

Marshmallow Fluff, like baking soda, is multitalented. It can be used as a sandwich spread in conjunction with peanut butter. The label features such recipes as, "Marshmallow Treats" and "Never-Fail Fudge." To the best of my knowledge, it's virtually impossible to make the fudge fail! For small change (25 cents as of this writing), Durkee-Mower, Inc. will send you a recipe book filled with all kinds of goodies you can make with Marshmallow Fluff. Oh, and Marshmallow Fluff has zero fat and is made only from egg whites, sugar, corn syrup, and vanillin. For Durkee-Mower's recipe book, write to: Lynne White, P. O. Box 470, Lynn, MA 01930. Check it out on the Internet at http://www.marshmallowfluff.com

Marshmallow Fluff will always have a special place in my heart. I once knew a guy named Steve who was no longer on the campus meal plan because he ran out of money. Every night you could find him in the computer lab with his trusty jar of the stuff. One jar kept Steve nourished for a week. I do not recommend copying Steve's dietary habits, but, considering that he stayed healthy, they do make for a nutritional mystery story!

PEANUT BUTTER

No discussion of Marshmallow Fluff would be complete without bringing up the topic of peanut butter. Low-fat peanut butter has around 6 grams of fat per tablespoon, while a tablespoon of regular peanut butter has 8½ grams of fat. However, the brand that I analyzed has both a reduced-fat and a regular version of its product on the market, but mysteriously both have the same 95 calories per tablespoon! The difference between the two versions was in the way the calories were distributed. In the low- fat peanut butter, 55 calories per tablespoon came from fat, while in the regular peanut butter 70 calories came from fat. This makes you wonder what goes on in the company's top secret product lab!

FRUIT COCKTAILS

In an attempt to add some variety to my college student diet, I tried snack-size canned fruit cocktails. They weren't as good as fresh fruit, of course, but nothing canned ever is. Not all fruit cocktails are created equal! There are two distinct categories: Fruit cocktails packed in heavy syrup and those packed in fruit juice or light syrup. Consider the following comparison of the same major national brand packed "heavy" and "light":

	Fruit Cocktail Comparision – National Brand	
	Heavy Syrup	*Lite in Fruit Juice*
Serving Size	127 grams	123 grams
Calories	100	60
Calories From Fat	0	0
Total Fat	0 grams	0 grams
Cholesterol	0 milligrams	0 milligrams
Sodium	10 milligrams	10 milligrams
Total Carbohydrates	24 grams	15 grams

Insanely, in both cases, the manufacturer's serving size was listed as half a can of fruit cocktail. Believe me, nobody ever eats half a can! The cans are tiny anyway! So in reality you might as well double the amount of calories. 100 calories become 200 per can with heavy syrup; and 60 calories become 120 with the light syrup. By eating the cocktail packed in light syrup, you're saving 80 empty calories! The tradeoff is that the lighter syrup is less sweet to the taste.

CHAPTER 6
ALCOHOL AND DRUGS

ALCOHOL

Alcohol is never in short supply in a freshman dorm. Somebody always has a friend who is at least 21 years old or who possesses a darn good fake identification card (ID). The only remaining problem is finding the time and place to consume the alcohol without getting caught.

As a college student you ought to be acquainted with some facts about alcohol. Alcohol is a depressant, which means that it is a sedative. An individual's tolerance for alcohol is determined mostly by a combination of the following factors: Weight, metabolism, gender, and food intake. Alcohol is reduced in the liver by an enzyme called dehydrogenase.

As a general rule-and this is not a sexist, but a physiological statement!-women tend to metabolize alcohol more slowly than do men and thus be more effected by it. This is because their bodies contain less dehydrogenase. In addition, the female hormone estrogen blocks the activity of dehydrogenase, while the male hormone androgen promotes it. This also explains why women experience a higher sensitivity towards alcohol right before their periods. All this is not to say, however, that there aren't women out there whose alcohol tolerance is greater than that of some men. Body hair, incidentally is a good indication of an individual's estrogen-androgen balance and, thus, alcohol tolerance. In other words, guys with very little chest hair are more likely to get plastered faster than do guys with a hairy chest.

There are many myths about alcohol that ought to be dispelled. Contrary to popular belief, a 1.5-ounce shot of hard liquor, a 5-ounce glass of wine, and a 12-ounce bottle of beer all HAVE THE SAME AMOUNT OF ALCOHOL. Infamous sayings such as, "Liquor, then beer—never fear" or "Beer, then liquor—never sicker" have no foundation in fact. There is no way to sober up quickly. Coffee doesn't work, nor does a cold shower. The best way to get rid of the effects of alcohol is to sleep it off.

Here are some facts that you might not have known about alcohol:

- **A 12-ounce bottle of beer averages about 150 calories. Imagine four beers in one night, that's 600 calories. I hope you like running laps around the gym, because otherwise you'll soon be on your way to a hefty beer gut.**
- **Light beer can vary from 70 to 140 calories per 12-ounce bottle. Oh by the way, the stuff tastes terrible. Don't believe the beer commercials, light beer is light in taste too.**
- **90-proof liquor is around 100 calories per 1.5 ounces. If you decide to do shots, remember those calories add up too.**
- **You can become more susceptible to the affects of alcohol if you are ill, fatigued, or emotionally stressed.**
- **If you want to know where you rank on the alcohol consumption barometer, consider that Americans (including babies and grannies) consume about 6 billion gallons of beer annually. This adds up to about 22 gallons per head per year. Because a gallon is almost two six-packs, the math says that, if you are "doing" more than one 12-ounce bottle of beer per day, you are exceeding the average!**

PARTIES

In case you didn't already know, the word party does not mean putting on silly hats, using noisemakers, eating cake, and yelling "Surprise!" In college, the term refers to the consumption of alcohol — lots of it. College freshmen are notorious party animals. Usually by your sophomore year the die-hard partygoers of your graduating class have either flunked out or been put on academic probation. Either way, for most students, freshman year is when their peers consume the most alcohol. College students have invented tons of methods of ingesting alcohol quickly and efficiently. Beer is the most popular example.

DRINKING GAMES

To make alcohol consumption easier and more pleasurable, college students often resort to drinking games. Unlike board games, video games, or even game shows, drinking games usually have no winner. Typically the only winning player is the one who chose not to play. Of all the drinking games played on college campuses, the types to avoid are endurance games. Endurance games are nothing more than an attempt to discover how much alcohol you can consume before you pass out. What often happens is that the players of these sadistic pastimes find themselves getting violently ill and vomiting into a toilet until the early hours of the morning. Beware of the following endurance games:

- **Century Club** - Every person takes a shot of beer once a minute, for 100 minutes. Not all players make it to 100 minutes. Consider that the average bottle of beer contains 12 ounces. So each shot is approximately 1.5 ounces. This means that, in 100 minutes, each player must drink about 150 ounces–or slightly more than two six-packs of beer. That's a lot of beer for anyone!
- **Keg Stand** - In this game each person tries to drink as much beer as possible, straight from the tap of a keg, without removing the mouth from the tap. A scorekeeper keeps track of how long each person holds on and swallows.
- **Sixty Seconds** - Players use a mechanical clock with a seconds hand. Each player is assigned a number (1 to 12 or 1 to 60). When the second hand strikes a person's number, he/she drinks his/her beer. The game goes on until there's no more beer, or everybody passes out.

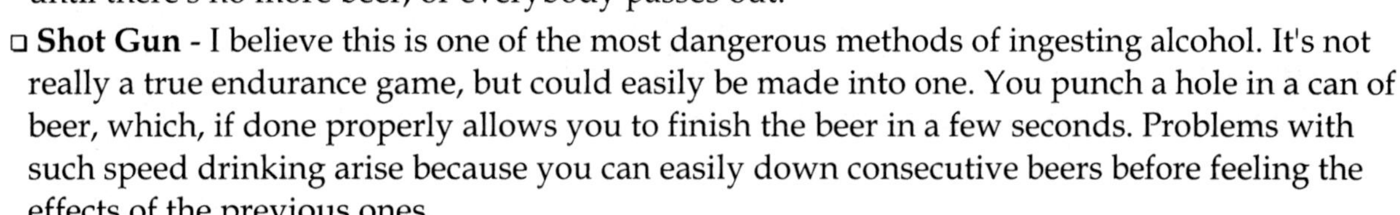

- **Shot Gun** - I believe this is one of the most dangerous methods of ingesting alcohol. It's not really a true endurance game, but could easily be made into one. You punch a hole in a can of beer, which, if done properly allows you to finish the beer in a few seconds. Problems with such speed drinking arise because you can easily down consecutive beers before feeling the effects of the previous ones.

Another party favorite you should know about is the Jell-O shot. Essentially it is Jell-O made with vodka and molded into the size of ice cubes. These shots are potentially dangerous, because the Jell-O flavoring effectively masks the taste of the alcohol and you can easily down too many of them and ingest more alcohol than you realize or is good for you.

SAINT PATRICK'S DAY

The day of the year that I dreaded more than exams or due days for projects was Saint Patrick's Day. Irish and non-Irish alike seem to celebrate this holiday with abandon. Our celebration took the form of long visits to my college town's bars. The bars opened early in the morning and didn't close until late at night. Twelve-hour drinking sprees were not uncommon. Lines leading up to the doorways of every bar formed early. The bars usually offered incentives (as if any were need!) to lure celebrators inside. These included leis, green beer, and party hats. The streets were filled with drunken and obnoxious people and the atmosphere was none too savory.

THE DANGER OF EXCESSIVE DRINKING

Excessive drinking on many college campuses has led to incidents of alcohol poisoning. Binge drinking is just not a defensible sport, under any circumstance! As with many other forms of poisoning, alcohol poisoning can be fatal. When a drinker's blood alcohol concentration (bac) creeps past .30, the danger accelerates. At around a .40 bac, alcohol poisoning can occur. A bac of .50 can be deadly! The signs of alcohol poisoning are:

- Clammy, cold, or blue-colored skin
- Difficulty breathing. Breathing slows to fewer than eight breaths a minute, or becomes erratic.
- Person has passed out and cannot be woken up.

If you suspect that a person might have alcohol poisoning, get help **IMMEDIATELY. DO NOT HESITATE**. Make sure the person is monitored all the time until help arrives. Turn the person onto his/her side so that if vomiting occurs, he/she won't inhale the vomit and choke on it.

ALCOHOL MISCHIEF AND MAYHEM

Students who drink sometimes get caught up in all kinds of crazy antics, and, in the process, make themselves easy prey for pranksters. If you pass out after too much booze, you could end up falling pray to any of these pranks:

- **Magic Marker Tattoos** People scribble all over you with a permanent magic marker.
- **Leg Shavings** Somebody will shave the hair off your legs.
- **Eyebrow Shaving** Somebody will shave off one or both of your eyebrows.
- **Ear Piercing** You could end up with an earring in your ear the hard way. Basically, somebody swabs your ear with alcohol and then pushes the pin of an earring through it.

THE FAKE ID

Obviously when you are 18, there is no legal way to purchase alcohol. A time-honored tradition for most underage drinkers is finding a darn good fake ID. Usually this takes the form of an out of state driver's license. Over the years driver's licenses have become much more sophisticated just to thwart such endeavors.

Here are some facts you might not have known about using a fake ID. In certain states minors can have their real license revoked for using a fake ID. A person purchasing a fake ID can be charged with perjury. In many states, the use of a fake ID is a felony. Unlike a misdemeanor, a felony means increased jail time, higher fines, and extended suspension of driving privileges. The worst part of being a felon is that you have a criminal record.

To add insult to injury, if you have a criminal record you might have a serious problem getting a job after college.

Now that I have completely scared you away from using a fake ID, want to know how one is spotted? This information is for educational use only - of course.

- **Photographs on licenses are taken with certain backgrounds. If the background doesn't match, that is a huge giveaway.**
- **Many licenses have holograms. Counterfeit holograms rarely match the legitimate ones 100%.**
- **The issue date on a license must match the expiration date in accordance with renewal interval for licenses in a particular state. In other words, if licenses are renewed every four years and the expiration date is five years after the issue date, you've got a big problem.**
- **Bad lamination is also a tip-off. If the license's lamination is peeling around the edges, it may be a fake.**
- **Fake licenses are often compared against the real deal for width, thickness and height.**
- **The bouncer/doorman will ask you to repeat to hm the details on your license such as the date of birth. If you stutter, your are instantly suspect.**
- **The most obvious giveaway on a fake license are your hair, eye color, and general appearance, if one or more of them don't match those of the person in the picture.**
- **Glues lines around the area of the picture or date of birth can also cause suspicion.**
- **The word "duplicate" on the license always invites extra scrutiny.**
- **An expired fake license is not likely to go undetected as a fake for long.**

Alcohol consumed in mass quantities creates something called the "Beer Goggles" effect. In short this means that, as you consume more alcohol, members of the opposite sex become increasingly more attractive. For guys this means that an indifferent-looking girl spotted while sober becomes an instant babe after a few beers. For girls this means that a lackluster guy can become a hunk. When you wake up the next morning and the alcohol wears off, you're in for a sudden, rude awakening! As the old saying goes, "There are no ugly girls at closing time."

DRINKING STORIES

What are drinking stories? I'm glad you asked. These are little tales about what happens to people who have consumed too much alcohol. Why am I writing about these? To both entertain and inform you. Because I lived in a college environment, where being outside was not a good idea for most of the year, drinking in dorms was often used to combat cabin fever.

Crazy Drinking Story #1

When my RA took off for the weekend, the craziness set in. (When that cat was away, the mice certainly did play!) Two guys on my floor got completely smashed. These two winners decided, after ingesting a case of beer, that they would drink another. When the second case was finished, they cut eye slits into the beer boxes and put them on their heads. Then they put on their roller blades and skated into the walls. They got pretty banged up, while the walls, of course, didn't even get scratched! I bet they wondered where those bumps on their heads came from the next morning.

Crazy Drinking Story #2

Every floor has an asshole. Pardon my language, but there is no better term. Our asshole turned into a bigger one when he got drunk. He would frequently do naughty things such as urinate on his roommate's chair, break furniture, and act generally obnoxious. One night asshole's roommate plotted revenge. Asshole passed out after a long night of drinking. The Roommate knew that asshole would be out cold and sleep like a board. As soon as asshole started snoring, his roommate took out the electric razor! He shaved off one of asshole's eyebrows and the hair off one leg. To perfect his revenge, he scribbled all over asshole's chest and face with a magic marker. The next morning, asshole awoke to an unpleasant surprise: Not only did he not remember the previous night's events, he also had no idea why he looked like he had lost a fight with a magic marker.

Crazy Drinking Story #3

After this humiliating experience, common sense would dictate that asshole would be more careful next time he got drunk. But again, asshole became careless and had one too many. This time, however, he didn't pass out. His roommate decided to try a little less subtle form of revenge. He stripped asshole to his underwear and handcuffed him to a railing. Apparently asshole had been cheating on his girlfriend. His roommate called asshole's mistress and had her come and pose next to the handcuffed asshole for a little photo session. Mysteriously, the photos ended up in the hands of asshole's girlfriend back home. For those who are curious, asshole did not return after sophomore year!

Crazy Drinking Story #4
A close friend of mine ended up in a situation that sounds like something out of an Alfred Hitchcock movie. Imagine this guy's surprise when he woke up one morning in a prison cell with a bandage on his hand!

Crazy Drinking Story #5
There is one thing that every college student should know: The night of your 21st birthday is a right-of-passage. Your friends will want to take you out for your first legal drink. You'll be asked to do all kinds of things like drink 21 shots or compete in a drinking contest. Either way, more than a few college students had to greet the first dawn of their maturity, the day after their 21st birthday, with a splitting headache and a stomach that felt as if they had swallowed an old shoe. One birthday dude got falling-down drunk on his 21st birthday, before suppertime. So he walked over to the cafeteria for a large meal. But he shouldn't have, because, no sooner had he finished eating that he had to throw up. None of the cafeteria employees would go near him to clean up the mess. In fact, for the entire remainder of the semester, they gave this dude the "evil eye" every time he ate in the cafeteria. He soon learned to order takeout food!

THE HANGOVER

The day after a night of drinking is when you truly pay the piper. If you drink heavily, it is inevitable that sooner or later you will wake up with a hangover. A hangover is often associated with a headache, nausea, and sensitivity to bright lights and loud noises. In short, the experience is not pleasant.

Hangovers are caused mostly by types of alcohol called fusel alcohols, such as methanol, propanol, butanol, isobutanol, and isoamyl alcohol. These taste almost solvent-like. Most of the alcohol in beer, wine, and spirits, however, is ethanol, which is the "good" alcohol that gives you less of a hangover.

It is important to understand that certain beverages, including wines, vodkas, and liqueurs, tend to contain more fusel alcohols than does beer, for instance, and are thus more likely to give you a hangover. The same applies to cheaper beverage brands, which tend to contain much larger amounts of fusel alcohols than do expensive, top-quality brands. Especially cheap vodkas can have so many fusel alcohols that you can taste them. So it is not the

types of drinks, but the types of alcohols in the drinks that determine whether or not you will get a hangover. The enzyme dehydrogenase in the liver reduces methanol to formaldehyde and, eventually, to ascorbic acid. It reduces the other fusel alcohols to acetaldehyde and finally to harmless acidic acid (vinegar). Both formaldehyde and acetaldehyde are poisons that slow down your heart and cause the brain to get less oxygen, with the resulting headache and nausea. A hangover usually lasts between 48 and 72 hours.

Note that dehydrogenase also occur in the stomach. So, if you drink a glass of wine after you have eaten a big meal that is high a carbohydrates, there is a chance that the wine will be absorbed and its alcohol will be reduced before it can reach your blood stream.

The common view that drinking different types of booze in one session is more likely to give you a hangover than drinking the same stuff all evening, therefore, is not true. In fact, if you drink the same type of beverage all night, such as a drink made with cheap vodka, and it is loaded with fusel alcohols, you are more likely to suffer for your sins the next day than if you had consumed many different types of top-quality drinks, but all with just ethanol. In other words, if you want to get your money's worth from your booze, it's always better to drink less but to drink better.

I've had my share of hangovers. No matter what anyone says - you will not see pink elephants. What you will do, is woof down ibuprofen, and lots of liquid. Your stomach will feel woozy for almost a full day. Nothing speeds up hangover recovery. Coffee or caffeine in general will help you function but they will not make you 100% efficient.

SOME ADVICE

Remember to practice common sense when you are partying. If something sounds like a bad idea to you, it probably is. Keep in mind that the drinking age in most states is 21. Colleges are becoming aggressively stricter in enforcing their alcohol policies. If they catch you with booze and you are under age, they can confiscate it and call your parents. If you're underage and you're caught drinking, you risk serious punishment. The last thing you want is to get expelled from college or arrested.

If you decide to drink, here are some warnings that you would be smart to heed:

- Never drink and drive.
- Never drink and roller blade.
- Never drink and go swimming, especially in abandoned quarries.
- Stay away from stairs, or if that is impossible, be very careful.
- Never drink on an empty stomach.

- ❑ Never mix medication or sleeping pills with alcohol.
- ❑ Stay away from cuckoo juice, a popular mixture at parties that consists of unknown liquids poured into a barrel by each guest.
- ❑ Stay away from straight grain alcohol, such as Ever Clear, which is nearly 180 proof. You can go blind.
- ❑ Watch out for friends who are intoxicated. Always walk drunken friends and associates home. You don't want them walking into harm's way while suffering from impaired judgment.

DRUGS

In high school you probably were forced to watch a zillion movies on the dangers of drugs in your health education class. You probably saw a movie that said something like, "Johnny did LSD. Now Johnny is in an institution. He never came off his high. Don't let this happen to you." Ok well there are the high school drug scare movies and the real world. I will attempt to bridge the two.

MARIJUANA

Marijuana is probably the most readily available illegal substance on most college campuses. It is easily detectable because of its distinct odor, which is similar to that of burning rope. Marijuana is the main reason why students burn incense—the incense covers up, so they hope, the smell of the drug before authority figures (such as the RA) notice.

Marijuana has many names: pot, grass, weed, herb, and reefer. Marijuana is comprised of portions of a hemp plant (*cannabis sativa*). Usually it contains a mixture of the leaves and flowers of the plant. Typically the drug is smoked in the form of a hand-rolled cigarette (a "joint"), or in a pipe (a "bong"). No matter how you smoke it, it smells awful.

The physical side effects of marijuana include:

- ❑ Loss of Balance
- ❑ Delayed Reaction
- ❑ Redness of Eyes

❑ Sleeping Difficulties
❑Reduced Coordination
❑ Accelerated Heartbeat (up to a 50% increase)

In addition to causing physical side effects, marijuana can affect your mental state and can cause:

❑ A Sense of Paranoia
❑ Anxiety
❑ Psychotic Impulses
❑ Depression

Keep in mind that marijuana can stay in your body for several days after have smoked it. It has been my observation that prolonged use of this drug causes people to begin neglecting their appearance. Personal hygiene suddenly becomes unimportant. After a smoking session, people get the munchies and will eat anything in sight! I also believe that marijuana leads to using of more serious drugs. I watched as people I knew were no longer satisfied with marijuana and began using LSD.

My junior year roommate was a major pothead. Amazingly, not only did he have an insatiable appetite for weed, but he also possessed one of the greatest intellects I have ever known. He could run circles around me academically, even while he was stoned. Life certainly isn't fair. However, all this talent did come at a price. He soon lost interest in going to classes, and began spending more and more of his time doing "other things." After graduation instead of becoming a premiere scientist, he took a menial job and never realized his full potential. Seemingly *cannabis sativa* robbed this individual of his goals and sense of drive.

LSD

Lysergic Acid Diethyl Amide (LSD) is on a comeback in college. LSD or "acid" is a hallucinogenic drug that is most commonly taken orally. The drug is often hidden in sugar cubes, half-centimeter blotter paper, pieces of candy, and capsules. Tabs are most often used, because they are easily hidden. Once ingested, it can take up to half an hour before the drug's effects set in. The process of going under the influence of LSD is referred to as a "trip." An acid trip can last as long as ten hours. When taken orally, LSD is absorbed in the gastrointestinal tract and works its way from there through the blood stream and into the brain. If a pregnant woman ingests the drug, it will also work its way to the

fetus.

In its virgin form, LSD is a white, odorless powder. It comes from a variety of places, including seeds of certain plants, fungi on certain grains, and drug labs. No matter what the source of LSD, it is ultimately a manufactured drug. It is either chemically refined from plants or completely synthesized in a laboratory. Either way, keep in mind that you are dealing with an illegally manufactured drug. It is impossible to determine how or who manufactured the drug. Remember that there are no safety standards in the manufacture of an illegal substance. In ingesting such contraband you are putting yourself at considerable risk.

Many people consider the effects of LSD to be mystical. Supposedly they see all kinds of images that don't exist outside their minds. Some LSD users claim that not only are their senses imbalanced, but they find it to be an immense source of creative inspiration, while others claim they can actually hear colors and see music.

But don't be fooled—it is not all pleasure. An adverse reaction to LSD is called "a bad trip" and the result can be disorienting. Once you have completed your trip, you may not be finished with the mind-altering effects of LSD! Flashbacks, a feeling that you are under the influence of LSD again, can occur as long as a year after your trip. In fact, a friend who was a chronic LSD user claimed to have had flashbacks nearly twenty years after his last trip! Flashbacks can last from seconds to hours.

While you are under the influence of LSD you may be subject to the following side effects:

- Hallucinations
- Sleeping Difficulties
- Lack of Appetite
- Raised Body Temperature
- High Blood Pressure
- Dilation of Pupils
- Tremors
- Chills
- Dizziness
- Sweating
- Decreased Coordination

In college I met more than a few LSD users. One particular user happened to be a senior year roommate. (I seemingly had the worst luck in roommates.) This fellow decided that his brain was meant for only one thing - frying like an egg. I watched one night as he came off of what must have been a bad trip. He yelled at me, "Get out of here! You're just too real [embodying too much reality] for me," after which he threw me out of the room. I guess the little green men that he kept seeing were giving him these orders.

I was not an LSD user. I have never tried it, nor was I tempted to. The idea of tweaking my mind into a chaotic state just never seemed appealing. However, some people felt that LSD provided them with the perfect dose of creativity for their otherwise mundane lives.

My thrill-seeking roommate bought thirty hits of LSD for senior week. (Thirty hits are equal to 300 hours of non-stop tripping!) Fortunately for his remaining brain cells, he decided to share the goodies with his friends. They sat in a large circle with the shades drawn. A set of strobe lights, mood music, and bottles with glowing fluorescent paint were arranged strategically in the room to enhance the quality of the trip. While under the influence, they composed a story that they claimed to be brilliant. To this day the story is completely unintelligible. I guess you have to be stoned to realize its brilliance! Shakespeare, these people were not!

CLUB DRUGS

A new class of drugs is gaining popularity on college campuses, nowadays. These drugs are categorized as club drugs. The name comes from the fact that these drugs are most commonly taken at high-energy dance clubs, trances, and rave parties.

ECSTASY

Ecstasy, whose chemical name is Methylenedioxymethamphetamine, also has other names, such as Adam, Clarity, Essence, Eve, Lover's Speed, MDMA, and XTC. Believe it or not, this drug started out with official credentials: A German chemical company once patented it, in 1913! It is now considered a designer drug, which means that it changes the molecular structure of an existing substance or drug. Since the drug does not occur naturally, it must be manufactured in a clandestine drug lab.

Typically Ecstasy is taken orally as either a tablet or a capsule. The drug is both a hallucinogenic and a stimulant. It combines the attributes of methamphetamine ("speed") with hallucinogenic properties. Unlike other drugs that just give you a high or a trip, this drug has other so-called endearing qualities. Many Ecstasy users claim that the drug allows them to dance energetically for hours, feel happiness, and empathy towards the people around them.

Unfortunately, these people would be telling you only one quarter of the story on

A quick note about clandestine drug labs: Unlike pharmaceutical companies that have large quality control departments, clandestine drug labs give what you get. There is no way of verifying that you bought what you paid for. You also do not know under which conditions the items were manufactured. Drug manufacture is an exact science, NOT GUESSWORK. You could just as easily be buying the end product of a crackpot, as you are a PHD. Those aren't the kind of odds I like to gamble on.

Ecstasy. First, Ecstasy can have some rather nasty side effects. These side effects include:

CLANDESTINE DRUG LAB

- Blurred Vision
- Chills
- Convulsions
- Faintness
- Accelerated Heart Rate
- High Blood Pressure
- Insomnia
- Loss of Appetite
- Involuntary Bowel Movements
- Muscle Tension
- Nausea
- Sweating
- Tremors

Second, Ecstasy can cause teeth grinding. People who take the drug sometimes use pacifiers and lollipops to counteract this nasty side effect. Imagine going to a nightclub and seeing people with pacifiers in their mouths!

Third, the half-life of Ecstasy is six hours. In six hours Ecstasy's effects are reduced by 50%. In 12 hours the effects are reduced by 25%, and so on. Finally after 48 hours the effects are completely worn off.

Fourth, when the drug wears off it can cause symptoms resembling a nasty hangover. It depletes the brain chemical seratonin, a compound that regulates aggressive behavior, eating and sleeping habits, sensitivity to pain, sexual function, and thought processes.

Finally, Ecstasy can cause long-term damage to your body. It can leave you with liver problems, a rash, and brain damage. In fact, monkeys that took the drug for four continuous days not only ended up with immediate brain damage, but the damage was still evident seven years later!

HERBAL ECSTASY

Don't let the name fool you. This stuff is no safer than the real thing! The drug is a mixture of inexpensive legal herbs. The key chemical ingredient is ephedrine. This chemical stimulates both the nervous and the cardiovascular system. Some of the typical names for Herbal Ecstasy are Cloud 9, GWM, Herbal Bliss, Herbal X, Ritual Spirit, and Ultimate Xphoria. Some of the nastier side effects of this drug include:

- Death
- Heart Attacks
- High Blood Pressure
- Seizures
- Strokes

GBH

GBH, Gamma-hydroxybutyrate, is a drug that often appears as an odorless and tasteless liquid. On occasion it has been known to appear as a white powder, tablet, or capsule. It is also called Cherry Meth, East Lay, Fantasy, G, Gamma 10, Georgia Home Boy, Gook, Grievous, G-Riffick, Liquid E, Nature's Quaalude, Organic Quaalude, Salty Water, Scoop, Soap, Somatomay, and Zonked. The drug causes both intoxication and deep sedation. It has been used as a date rape drug. The effects set in within 20 minutes and can last up to four hours. The side effects include:

- Delusions
- Depression
- Nausea
- Seizures
- Unconsciousness
- Vertigo
- Vomiting

Why anybody would want to voluntarily use this drug is beyond me. I am told that it is popular at Raves. The drug is often manufactured with recipes found on the Internet. That fact alone should make you worry about using it! Making matters worse, emergency rooms have a hard time detecting this drug for treatment. Stay away, stay far away from this stuff!

KETAMINE

This drug is typically used by veterinarians as an animal anesthetic. It is rarely used in

human medicine except under illegal circumstances. The common slang names for this drug are Cat Valium, Special K, Vitamin K. The drug is often available either as a liquid or powder. It can be smoked or snorted. The side effects include:

- Delirium
- Depression

ROHYPNOL

This drug is a real bad boy. It is often used for date rape and has been called "the forget-me pill." On the street it has such names as La Roche, R2, Rib, Roachies, Rope, Rophies, and Roofenol. This drug is also available in liquid and powder forms. It is illegal in the United States and not available by prescription. However, it is approved overseas for treatment of such illnesses as insomnia. The really scary part of using this drug is that those who take it (voluntarily or involuntarily) may not remember events experienced while under this drug's influence. This stuff is just such bad news, only a moron would take it voluntarily. I offer this warning, at clubs, watch your drinks, and make sure nobody slips this stuff into it! Don't take drinks from people you don't know or have just met. You might find yourself the next day someplace with no recollection of how you got there and what you did while you were there.

CHAPTER 7
BOOK BUYING

I remember how excited I was to receive a $500 scholarship during award night in high school. My newly gained financial windfall was not only going to pay for all my books, but get me some new clothes, too. Wrong! That money barely paid for my first semester's books. Boy, was I naïve!

BOOKSTORE MONOPOLY

Most colleges have an officially sanctioned bookstore. The nature of the connection of this bookstore to the college is not clear. My personal suspicion is that the bookstore not only pays rent to the college but also pays a percentage of the income back to the school.

In many cases, the campus bookstore has a virtual monopoly on book selling, especially if the college is in a small town or city where it's either too inconvenient or plain impossible to go elsewhere. Other stores would most likely have to order the books you need so you might not have them in time for your first assignments. Since the professors provide their reading lists to the campus bookstore before the beginning of a semester, you are virtually guaranteed that the store has most of the books you need in stock when classes start.

Since the big, bad campus bookstore is the only game in town, it should come as no surprise that it often shows no shame in pricing. A friend of mine from another college once needed an expensive hardcover textbook for one of his classes. His campus bookstore's price was so high, he drove to the closest bookstore of the same national chain where, to his amazement, he found the same book for 20% less. On campuses the college bookstore has been renamed "college crookstore".

So here's the dirt on how the money from the retail sale of a typical textbook is split up: According to figures provided by the National Association of College Stores, about 65% of the retail price goes to the publisher.. So where does the rest of the money go? Good question! The author gets only about 11.5%. The bookstore takes the remaining 23.5%, twice as much as the person who wrote the book! And about five-sixths of that 23.5% is eaten up by the bookstore's overhead (personnel, store operations and freight). This leaves the campus bookstore with about a 4% pretax profit off the retail price you pay for your textbook.

When a competing bookstore opened in my college town, it did not receive booklists from the college or professors so it could not pre-order books to give students a choice of vendor. It was rumored amongst the students that the college issued a memo to the faculty that under no circumstances were booklists to be given to "the competition." Students could neither confirm nor deny the existence of this memo, but within a few weeks every professor on campus provided the new store with a booklist, thereby effectively removing a monopoly that had existed for years!

ON-LINE BOOKSTORES TO THE RESCUE

With the advent of the Internet, students now have more choices for textbook purchases. On-line bookstores in many cases can charge lower prices for books because their overhead is lower. All the on-line bookstore has to do is ship from their warehouse to your campus mailbox. So the big bad campus bookstore no longer has the upper hand! However, there is one slight drawback, you have to order your books early enough that you will receive them before classes start.

To get an idea how on-line bookstores compare, examine the table below. It contains price comparisons for the book "Computer Graphics: Principles and Practice in C" ISBN: 0201848406. This book is a standard textbook used in computer science courses. The total cost is based on the cheapest possible delivery method. The same book would cost you about $75.00 in a campus bookstore.

Consider the following comparison of on-line bookstores:

Bookstore	Book Price	Shipping Method	Shipping Price	Total Cost
www.amazon.com	$74.99	Standard Ground 3 to 7 business days	$3.00 + .99 for book	$78.98
www.barnesnoble.com	$74.99	Standard Ground 3 to 6 business days	$3.00 + .99 for book	$78.98
www.ecampus.com	$71.25	UPS Ground 1 to 5 business days	$2.99 + .99 for book	$75.23
www.varsitybooks.com	$74.95	UPS Ground 3 to 5 business days	$3.95 + 3% of order	$81.15
www.doublediscount.com	$58.57	USPS 5 to 9 business days	$1.00 + $3.50 for item	$63.07
www.textbookx.com	$63.83	USPS 4 to 14 business days	$2.49 + .99 for book	$67.31

Also note that there is often some flexibility in the price and the shipping charges. The amounts for shipping listed here are the ones listed on the website, but there are often special deals on shipping if you spend more than a certain amount. In fact, sometimes you can get shipping for free. At least one of these websites always seems to be running a deal or a special.

Keep in mind that it is very easy to comparison-shop on the Internet. One website specializes in just finding the best deal on products that are available on the Internet. It is called www.bizrate.com. You can use this website to find bargains on college textbooks as well.

CAMPUS BOOKSTORE WEIRDNESS

As I mentioned earlier, the exact connection between the bookstore and the college is murky at best. Here is a particular example that really drives that message home. A major gripe I had with the campus bookstore was the issue of study supplements. In high school, when I was assigned classic literature I used Cliff Notes. *The Canterbury Tales,* written in Middle English, was a significant change of pace from the pulp fiction I was used to reading, and Cliff Notes allowed me to figure out the cryptic passages and enhance my comprehension. My college bookstore, however, conveniently neglected to carry Cliff, Baron, or Monarch Notes for any of the classic literature on my booklists. I had to have my Cliff Notes sent to me from home.

Dumbfounded as to the rationale behind such commercial craziness (after all, there was an obvious demand unmet by supply), I interrogated someone, who worked in the bowels of the campus bookstore, to get to the bottom of this. After some arm-twisting, I finally got this answer: "The decision not to carry these supplemental aides is a prime example of the symbiotic relationship between the college and its on-campus bookstore. College administrators and/or some of the professors view these works as substitutes that allow students not to read the full, required text. Therefore, they frown upon such aids.And while they cannot actually ban the sale of these supplemental aides, by not letting them into the campus bookstore they manage to actively discourage them."

BUYING USED BOOKS

Without a doubt, the biggest rip-offs at the campus bookstore are its buyback practices for used books. This is the definitive sucker's game, in my opinion. The bookstore generally offers a used version of many of the texts on your booklist. A used book is usually well worn, marked with highlights, underlined, and has a weak or damaged binding. You will pay less for it, than if it were new, but not that much less, and it won't last as long.

There are three major drawbacks to buying a used book:

- If you want to resell it, you will get little money for it, or you can't resell it at all.

- The edition you buy may be out of date. (Publishers put out new editions at an alarming rate, often every second or third year, especially if the book is for a popular introductory class, such as Economics 101 or Psychology 101.)
- Because used books already have a lot of mileage on them, they might not last another four years of college. This becomes an issue if the book is an introductory text that is relevant to your major. Sometimes the book won't even last a semester!

At the end of the semester, your so-called friends at the campus bookstore will offer a buyback program. Remember how you spent all that money for textbooks at the beginning of the semester? The bookstore will now offer to buy back those books at 25% or less of what you originally paid for them. It will then resell them as used for between 50 and 75% of the original cost!

The following example shows you what a racket that is:

Say, you pay $100 for a new book. At the end of the semester, you sell it back to the bookstore for $25. So the bookstore got $75 of your money. ($100 - $25 = $75). The bookstore resells the book used for $50. By now, the bookstore has made $125 on YOUR book: $75 + $50 = $125. The student who bought your book used sells it back to the bookstore at the end of the semester for $25. The bookstore can now resell the book again as used for $50. This adds up to $125 - $25 + $50 = $150. So the bookstore has now made a total of $150 from YOUR original book, which you no longer own.

This cycle continues until either the book disintegrates or the professor changes to a new edition or to a different text. During my freshman year I bought my Physics 101 textbook for $50 used. In my senior year, the professor unfortunately decided to switch to the new edition that had just come out. The campus bookstore had piles of my textbook in the bargain bin for 98 cents!

My advice is to sell your books back to the store only if you absolutely need the money. Only sell books that are not related to your major in any way! If you do choose to sell back your books, consider the sage maintenance advice a friend of mine has to offer: "Be sure not to write in your books. They [the bookstore] will not allow you to sell them back as used books if you do."

GENERAL RULES OF THUMB

If you are going to buy your books on campus, do it as early as possible because everybody else will be buying theirs, too! Lines can get long and sometimes books sell out, especially if the class is popular or the bookstore receives an inaccurate head count. By buying early, you'll likely avoid both problems. One freshman warned me: "If they [the bookstore] run out of texts for classes, you could be on the waiting list for two weeks." Another thing to keep in mind when buying books is not to pay cash. Why? Simple, you don't know how much the books are going to cost. Your best method of payment is by check or credit card.

If you decide to buy your books on-line you will also want to order them early. Depending on the type of shipping you can afford, you may have to wait a while for your books to arrive. The last thing you want is for your books to arrive after classes have started.

When you've got all your books, make sure you put your name in each of them, in ink! Your most valuable possessions are your books and notebooks. Never leave them unattended in libraries, study lounges, or the cafeteria. A friend of mine once left the door to his room open while he went to check his mailbox. When he returned, all his textbooks were gone! Never lend your books or notebooks to anybody. NEVER. Do not put them into baggage. You cannot afford for some gorilla in the luggage department to lose them!

In addition to purchasing textbooks, you may be required to purchase a lab notebook for such classes as chemistry or physics. A lab notebook is usually spiral bound with both line and graph paper. Always buy more than one notebook for your lab classes! First, if you lose one you'll have a spare. Second, if you run out of space in the first notebook you can continue in the second. Third, some professors have strict rules about what you can and cannot write into a lab notebook. One of my professors had all these outlandish rules about crossing out errors. To outwit him, I used a spare lab notebook during class and copied the results neatly into another notebook, which I then handed in to be graded.

PROBLEM SOLVERS

Sometimes your campus bookstore will offer books such as *Thousands of Problems in* [Differential Equations, Calculus, Chemistry, etc.] *Solved*, which I found to be not only expensive but also useless! They aren't much help for the following reasons:

- The methods used to solve the problem may differ from those the professor or your textbook uses. You don't have time to learn more methods than you are already being taught, especially if they are not really relevant.
- The examples in the problem solver may not apply to your homework assignment.
- Since the professor will most likely only use your text and homework assignments as exam source material, purchasing the book may be a complete waste of money.

MISCELLANEOUS ITEMS

Campus bookstores usually carry other items besides books. You can also find official school T-shirts, sweatshirts, beer glasses, mugs, key rings, and drink warmers. In fact, some stores resemble a miniature department store. One student griped, "Before a national chain took over our campus bookstore it was like a department store. I could use my personal points [campus monetary system] to buy all kinds of things such as makeup." One bookstore even operates a full coffee shop on its premises.

Finally, there is one thing that you should never buy at a campus

bookstore—stationary supplies. The prices you'll pay for such necessities as pen, paper, and erasers are so high, you'll soon find yourself broke! Always buy those items off campus.

CHAPTER 8
WHAT YOU NEED TO KNOW ABOUT THE EDUCATION PROCESS

THE EDUCATION PROCESS

CLASSES

College classes work a little differently from high school classes. For science, business, and humanities classes, you need to go to a large hall or auditorium approximately two or three times a week to hear the professor give a lecture. In addition, once a week, you have a session with a teaching assistant (TA), usually a graduate student, to go over the homework assignment. This is your opportunity to ask questions about those parts of the assignment that are unclear to you.

Literature classes, on the other hand, tend to be more informal and discussion-based. You usually meet the professor in a room with 20 to 40 other students to discuss the week's readings. A significant portion of your grade will depend on how well you participate in these discussions. Be on your toes! Professors love to throw curve-ball questions that are almost impossible to answer. Remember to take copious notes during these sessions. Any passage the professor discusses could appear on exams or be chosen as the topic of a paper.

One thing you will realize quickly about all classes in college: Professors DO NOT spoon-feed you material the way your high school teachers did, and you'll discover that self-reliance is your best teacher. Don't depend on the professor to make the material clear to you. It is your responsibility to find a way to learn and to overcome any difficulties!

NOTETAKING

Unless you're a genius with a photographic memory, you'll need to take notes. Tape recorders do not work all the time, particularly in a large lecture hall, where there might be too much echo or the professor is too far away for your recorder to pick up

the audio. But the never-fail method is notes by penmanship.

Of course, I did know students who never took notes. Some of them had 4.0s-obviously the result of Mensa-level IQs and near-photographic memories. Unless you fall into that category, spend some money on pen and paper.

In four years of college I've tried every notebook type there is. I finally put together a system that worked for me: Start out with one spiral-bound five-subject notebook for each of your classes. Make sure it has perforated pages and is three-hole punched. Never buy a single-subject notebook. Why? It never holds enough paper for a whole semester, especially if you write in large letters as I do.

Then buy a loose-leaf notebook for each of your classes. Write your day-to-day notes in the spiral-bound book and, at the end of the day, tear the pages out and place them in the appropriate loose-leaf binders for your classes. Collect all exams, assignments, and handouts in the same binder. Investing in a three-hole punch is definitely worthwhile, because much of the material you receive is not punched. This way, everything is well organized, easy to find, and you won't lose a thing.

Warning! Do NOT lend your notes to ANYBODY! They are often more valuable than your textbooks. Without your notes, you could lose an entire semester's work. Write your name, phone number, student ID number, and campus address inside each notebook. Also, when you take an airplane never place your notebooks in your checked luggage if. They belong in your carry-on bag!

THE EXAM

After all the lectures, notes, and quizzes comes the inevitable exam. Every exam has its pratfalls. To ensure that there are no surprises, read about the six types below and be prepared.

- **Written exam for a literature class.** This exam consists of essay questions that must be answered in little blue notebooks. Most of the topics come straight from class discussions, homework, or the literary works themselves. Always cite generously from the sources to back up your statements.
- **Calculative exams** (math, science, certain business classes). Make sure you show all your work on these exams. Most professors will give you at least partial credit for setting up the proper equation or using the correct formula, even if your answer is not correct.
- **Multiple choice exams.** These are the worst exams of all. The professor usually has seen every possible wrong answer on exams taken by students who have gone before you. The professor often collects these wrong answers as material for his multiple-choice exams. These exams are nasty because you usually get no points for partial answers, and you're often given a penalty for guessing incorrectly.
- **Oral exams.** I've only had one of these. The professor questioned each student in his office for about 20 minutes to find out what he or she knew. For me the experience was nerve wracking! I felt as though the professor was scrutinizing every word I spoke. Fortunately, the professor was aware of how nervous I was and gave a fair exam with few trick questions.
- **Group exam.** I don't know of anybody else who has ever taken one of these. The premise behind group exams is that if many students do poorly in the class, they should be allowed to take the exam in groups of two. My partner and I failed, partly because we spent more time trying to communicate with each other than dividing and conquering the problems. The exam became a test of our cooperation and division of labor instead of our knowledge of the course material.
- **Open-book exam.** Believe it or not, this is one of the harder types of exam. Because you have the book in front of you, you can't get partial credit for copying formulas, dates, or constants. Don't be fooled into thinking that because the answers are in front of you, you don't have to study beforehand. If you spend all your time looking things up, you'll never finish the exam. Think of the book as a crutch that you can lean on when trouble arises. Prepare the book for the exam. Highlight important passages. Stick tags in the crucial chapters so that you can open right to them. This will also help you study more effectively. But, of course, writing in the book will reduce its resale value.

Here are some hints on how to increase your exam score:

- **Pace yourself.**
- **Always double-check your work before handing it in. You'd be surprised how many silly mistakes you can make, such as simple errors in arithmetic.**
- **Solve the easy problems first and save the harder ones for last.**
- **Don't give up! Never hand in a blank exam! Show that you made an effort. I once was clueless in an Applied Algebra exam. I couldn't figure out the first part of a multipart problem. Rather than give up, I wrote down what I would do if I had been able to solve the first part of the problem. The professor gave me a 98! I aced the exam!**

CHEAT SHEETS

Sometimes professors will allow you to have "cheat sheets" during an exam. These are sheets of paper on which you can write formulas, equations, and homework problems. The hidden agenda behind all of this is that by creating such a sheet you are actually studying the material. My cheat sheets were the stuff of legend. I crammed an entire semester's worth of work in the tiniest block lettering onto a single page. Ironically, my cheat sheets became so good that, when I allowed friends to use them, they sometimes got higher grades than I did!

Tip: To write really small letters you need a very sharp pencil. Never use a mechanical pencil, because the lead smudges.

PROJECTS

In addition to exams, some courses require you to complete a project, which will comprise a significant portion of your grade. Usually such a project is assigned for the duration of the semester. BUT DON'T WAIT UNTIL THE LAST MINUTE TO START IT! Remember that most of your projects will be due the same week, mostly because every professor believes that you only worry about his or her class! If you don't work on these projects incrementally during the semester, you probably won't get much sleep the week everything is due!

Also keep in mind that projects can evolve over time. Professors often discover that because of time, resource availability, or other extraneous factors, certain parts of the project may be unrealistic to complete in a single semester. Therefore, he or she might change the requirements on the fly. You should keep up to date with these changes so you don't find yourself doing extra work and suffering unnecessary stress.

WORKING WITH OTHER STUDENTS

Want to know the worst part of the college experience? Learning to work with your fellow college students on a project, that's what. This is the reason why professors often make you work with a lab partner or in a group as part of your semester project.

A group is only as strong as its weakest member. The most common problem with any group is that inevitably one or more members don't perform his or her fair share of the work. This means you've got to take up the slack, if you want a decent grade.

Professors claim that you should let them know if a problem arises. Supposedly they want you to make it clear that the work presented was an equal effort. In fact, some professors go so far as make you sign a document claiming you did your share. But we don't live in an ideal world. You shouldn't be surprised if somebody slacks. And if your lab or group partners are friends, it is very difficult to rat them out. Nobody wants to be known as a snitch.

Just like the question on a popular game show, "Who is the weakest link?", I've met my fair share. In lab classes I had my grades undermined by 4.0 students who had superior book smarts but no common sense. One such moron left me holding the bag about 4:00 a.m. on the day the lab was due. Oh and by the way, with whom did the professor sympathize? Not with me! After all I wasn't the 4.0 student and darling of the class. I had to finish the work myself and squeaked out a grade just above passing!

LIBERAL STUDIES CLASSES

Most freshmen are required to take some sort of general literature class, which covers such topics as classic literature, philosophy, and ethics. Look at such literature classes as an opportunity to get a 4.0 in at least one class. This doesn't mean they are "blow-off" affairs, but unlike most classes, if you put in a decent amount of work you CAN get a top grade.

Professors will give you a set of criteria to evaluate. You will be required to evaluate such items as plots, characters, and themes. Become familiar with these criteria because they are likely to be the basis of most papers, discussions, and exam questions. For example, some professors are so fascinated with the concept of the tragic hero that they seek out this character in every work of literature they assign.

Pay attention to any passage the professor goes over in class. These are the passages that the professor feels are important. Familiarize yourself with them so that you can recognize quotations from them. Write down all related discussions. This material may come in handy for exams and essay questions.

For classic literature assignments buy both Cliff Notes and Monarch Notes. Use the notes to review the passages you're currently working on BEFORE classes and quizzes. The notes are not a substitute for reading the actual material, but they can help you understand stories and poems written in archaic English. They also outline key plot points.

Quizzes tend to be fact based. Such things as character names and plot elements are fair game. Exams are normally in essay form and often require you to repeat class discussions.

Papers are a bit trickier. Many literature professors require that you write two or three papers a semester. You don't have to be a terrific writer to get a good grade, but you do have to prove your point. These papers are like the essays you wrote in high school. You should have a topic sentence and several supporting paragraphs. Your paper should have the following form:

Introduction:
This should be no longer than one paragraph. It introduces the topic and states your thesis (your position or opinion) and describes what you intend to prove in the paper.

Supporting paragraphs (body):
Begin each paragraph with an appropriate transition such as:

To begin,
Furthermore,
Moreover,
Therefore,

The support paragraphs comprise the ***Body*** of your essay. The first sentence should be a statement of proof for your thesis. After the first sentence, cite specific examples from the text to back up the paragraph's initial statement. Use quotes or paraphrase as necessary, but be sure to indicate where you got your material (you don't want to be accused of plagiarism).

Conclusion:
Use this section to summarize your proof, and finally, restate your thesis.

What I've outlined above is not the most elegant formula for a paper, but it is simple and straightforward. When you are proving your point, try to cite as many specific examples as possible. Remember that it's easier to write a critical or negative paper than a positive one.

Always use a word processor for your papers. Never write them by hand. Use the spacing and formatting the professor has requested, and always spell check the paper before you print it out.

BUYING A PAPER OR ESSAY

For whatever reason, some students just don't want to write their own essays. Perhaps they feel they lack the ability to write well or maybe they are just lazy. Either way, in case you lived under a rock in a remote section of the galaxy, it is possible to buy papers on the Internet.

Internet term paper sites are often called *paper mills*. The quality of the papers these sites offer varies as much as their cost. There are two types of bought papers: off-the-shelf and custom. Purchasing a custom paper means that the paper mill has to pay somebody on its staff to write a paper just for you, and that gets expensive. Currently 17 states have made it illegal to sell papers to students. More importantly, using a bought paper is cheating and violates the school's academic honesty policy.

HOW THE PROFESSOR WILL PREVENT YOU FROM USING A BOUGHT PAPER

- The professor will ask for interim outlines of the paper you plan to submit.
- Aligning all paper topics very close to the specific purpose of the course. This way there is little likelihood that a generic paper exists that deals with the topic the professor has chosen.
- Asking students obscure questions such as "why did this particular situation NOT happen." Where there are tons of papers available on "why something happened" there are bound to be fewer papers on the inverse.

PROFESSORS

THE GAMES THEY PLAY

Professors use all kinds of scare tactics to get students to take their classes seriously. Some take attendance while others play head games. The latter group is the one to look out for.

Often these so-called "head-trip professors" will make most of their students believe they are going to fail, and students often drop out of their classes like flies. Sometimes as much as half a class can disappear during a semester. I believe that professors do this on purpose to weed out students who are just filling their schedules. This leaves only dedicated students with a real interest in the subject.

Remember that, no matter how difficult an exam or assignment might be, somebody will always get a high grade, either by luck, skill, or smarts. Learn to accept this.

Many professors keep exam grades low deliberately. They may even have established in advance the number of As, Bs, Cs, Ds, and Fs they want to hand out. These professors make you earn your grades through blood, sweat, and tears.

Some professors claim there is no curve and that they will fail the entire class if necessary. The truth is, if they fail everybody, somebody will notice. The students would protest, and colleges hate negative press. More importantly, the dean of the department (the professor's boss) doesn't want to deal with such silliness. When a professor fails the whole class, it really means that he or she failed to teach the course properly. The dean (and indeed the professor) knows it, too. This means that professors cannot flunk everyone or even the majority without creating a negative reflection on their professional career. Professors who have tried to perpetrate massive flunking mysteriously vanish from the faculty roster a year or two later. Therefore, when the majority of the class is about to fail, the professor is likely to offer some kind of last-minute deal to help more students pass. I believe this tactic is planned months ahead of time and is part of the professor's master plan.

The deal often works like this: Course grades are cumulative. If you do better in the final exam on a topic that was already covered in a mid-term exam, the professor may average the two scores or replace the original score with the higher one. Don't go into the final expecting it to be easier than any of the previous exams, but the professor will often give you problems similar to those with which caused the class difficulties the first time. This way the professor can track if the students have learned from their mistakes and finally mastered the material.

PROFESSORS DON'T ALWAYS HAVE THE UPPER HAND

Some professors may strike you as intimidating. They may make it look impossible to get a passing grade, or they just can't teach. Believe it or not, incompetent professors do get tenure, too. Sometimes it is "whom you know, not what you know." Always remind yourself that your tuition helps pay your professor's salary. As a paying customer you are entitled to a certain level of service. Ask yourself, "Did I get fair value for my money?" If the answer is "NO," you have recourse!

Consider this situation, in which the student got the best of his professor:

A friend of mine took a summer course in a computer language. The instructor was a graduate student with very limited teaching experience, and he was far from being up to the task of teaching a complex programming language to a group of underclassmen. My friend put in a tremendous effort to pass the class, but he still failed the exams. However, it was his professor who performed the real failure. The professor failed to teach my friend the material. Instead of accepting an "F" on his transcript, my buddy contested the class and the tuition to the Dean of Computer Science! After telling the dean, "This professor couldn't teach his way out of a wet paper bag," my friend not only got his money back, but the grade was removed from his transcript! Sometimes it pays to consult a higher authority.

Occasionally a professor just can't teach you, and you alone. Not everybody on this planet is on the same wavelength. Some professors got lost in a time warp, or they never came off the acid they did in 1968. No matter, it is possible to reach academic gridlock. Academic gridlock occurs when you've repeated the same class with the same professor and still can't get a passing grade. At this point you should throw in the towel. Don't give up passing the class, but give up trying to pass this professor's class.

One senior I knew had a professor, who was known to be a bastard. (Hey, the word fits so I am going to use it.) This professor, who was also the department chair, made it his personal quest to be the gatekeeper to any undergraduate getting a degree. The poor senior took a class three times with "the bastard," because he was the only professor on campus who taught this class. So it became clear to the professor that this student would never give up, but would keep coming to his class until he passed. So the professor finally gave in and allowed the student to take the class off campus from another professor!

EVALUATING THE PROFESSOR

to answer questions during exams! If an exam question was unclear or even if it had a misprint (which could make a trivial problem impossible to solve), too bad! He would make us wait until the day the exam was handed back before answering any questions. However, this did not mean that he changed our exam grades if we found fault with an exam! To add insult to injury, on the day evaluation forms were handed out; he wouldn't leave the lecture hall!

Another professor whom I felt worthy of a reprimand was my Quantum Physics professor. Although he knew his material, he was a very ineffective teacher. It is noteworthy to point out that this professor was considered a brilliant scientist. However, part of being a good professor is having a rapport with the students. This guy never spoke to students before or after lectures! The moment the lecture was over, he bolted out of the room. (Often he did this before we could ask questions on homework assignments!) Ironically, after all the students gave him a negative evaluation, he did not return to teach Quantum Physics the following year.

There are some professors worthy of praise, who go the extra mile for students, and they deserve both compensation and recognition. For example, one of my professors encouraged students to call him at home if necessary, and another offered to hold additional review sessions at night. I made sure that I gave these professors good reviews.

Dealing with Professors Who Lack Fluency in English

This is where I get accused of being not "politically correct." So be it! Many times colleges and universities need professors with specialized knowledge to teach certain classes. Unfortunately, such knowledge may be scarce and the school may not have many applicants to choose from. Often the professors they hire have a very limited command of the English language. This does NOT mean these professors don't know their subjects, but it does mean you WILL have difficulty understanding what they say. Most likely you will have a hard time

It seemed to me that my college always assigned professors with the least fluency in English to the most difficult classes. This once cost me a passing grade.

One professor, who taught in the largest lecture hall on campus, had difficulty pronouncing words containing the letter 'X.' The further back in the lecture hall I sat the more garbled his words became. After a while all I could hear was gibberish. Front-row seats were almost impossible to get. They were in high demand, because only there could you comprehend what was being said. I failed the class largely because I couldn't get one word from the class lectures. Other students were in the same boat. So we all flooded his office, which made his office hours useless, too. Nearly 40% of his class failed.

Most of my friends got Ds. I took the class a second time with a professor who spoke fluent English and got a decent grade. However, the fact that I had to retake the class put me behind in my coursework and almost prevented me from graduating on time.

learning from them.

Classes are stressful enough on their own. The last thing you need is an obstacle such as a language barrier that prevents you from absorbing the material. I really wish colleges and universities would test the speaking ability of their faculty before they let them loose on students! That's outright carelessness and irresponsibility on the part of the school. School is just too costly to put up with this kind of fraudulent poor service.

MAKING THE GRADE

Every year I hear a new crop of freshmen say something like, "My professor is a jerk," or "My professor doesn't care if he flunks the entire class." Listen, there's something you should know. Many professors deliberately keep the grades low so that they can use a curve at the end of the semester. Not only that, they make the exams excruciatingly hard to challenge you to use every bit of knowledge you have to get a flunking grade without the curve. In the following paragraphs I outline the tricks and tips that I used to keep my grades above sea level.

Always show up for class. It doesn't matter if the professor takes attendance or not. Always sit in the first few rows, if you can get a seat there. This makes your face known to the professor. It will show that you have an interest in the class. When it comes time to get help or a better grade, the professor will be more sympathetic to you.

I once took a class in Software Systems. Before the last hour exam I had both a decent homework and test average. However, I bombed the exam so badly that no matter what I did the rest of the semester I wouldn't be able to get a decent grade in the class. Naturally I decided to see the professor. I explained my plight to him. Amazingly he said this to me: "Kid, your grades are usually better than this exam. I'll tell you what, you attend class regularly—I know you're trying. Let me raise your exam grade to a 65; that way you have a chance to still get a good grade in my class." I ended up with a 3.0 in the class thanks to my sympathetic professor.

By sitting in the front row of the lecture hall, you force yourself to pay attention. Sitting way back in the last row makes it too easy to doze off or daydream. Also, if you're near sighted, as I am, you don't want to spend 45 minutes to an hour squinting or missing important notes because you can't read the board.

One of my professors took particular relish in finding students who slept during his lectures. He would climb into the rows of students, drop a quarter on the sleeping student's desk and say, "Here, go buy yourself a cup of coffee!" The laughter from the class would wake the student up.

Another item to keep in mind is that homework *counts*. In some classes it could count as much as 20% of your grade. You'd be foolish not to do it.

Always show up to the last class before the hour exam. Usually the professor outlines what will be on the exam and often lets a hint slip. In fact, I once had a professor who actually told us exactly what kind of problems would be on the exam. This way I didn't waste effort studying useless data. Another professor used to say, "If you know this... this…and this…you've got a hundred. That's it." I got a 4.0 in his class.

The other wild card you can play to keep your grade level respectable is to take advantage of professors' office hours and tutors. Most professors hold office hours, which are posted at the beginning of the course, to talk to students one-on-one and answer questions. I learned more from dealing with the professor at this level, and I benefited from the added attention. This also lets the professor put a face to your name when deciding grades for the semester.

One of my professors who taught Electrical Science was from India and was difficult to understand in the large lecture hall. When I met him one-on-one not only was he exceptionally amiable, but he was much easier to understand. When I showed concern for his course, he showed concern for me. I didn't pass his class, but I found going to him was very helpful.

Tutors were invaluable in allowing me to finally pass Electrical Science and get a respectable grade in my Quantum Physics class. Tutors are usually upperclassmen or graduate students who have already taken the course and got at least a 3.0. Often they have insight into the class and the professor who is teaching the class (more importantly, they can give you their old exams from which to study).

The last great trick concerns old exams. There are standard classes, such as Calculus 101, which tons of people have taken before you. Most upperclassmen save their old exams. Old exams give you an idea what to expect on the hourly exam and let you practice your answers. Most professors change their exams only slightly, sometimes just the format, often asking the same type of questions year after year.

CHEATING

This topic is probably the one dearest to many hearts. Who hasn't felt the temptation to get even with the very system that has been putting them down. I've been tempted many times, but in the end, I NEVER CHEATED ON AN EXAM. The stakes were just too high. Did I ever copy homework? Yes, guilty as charged. Do I recommend it, NO!

So, what would you like to know about cheating? First, let me tell you why NOT to cheat. Then if you are still reading I'll spill some dirt on the topic.

Many colleges have an honor code that you, the student, are required to sign. The code outlines rules and principles of academic honesty. By signing this document you agree to uphold these rules and acknowledge the consequences for breaking them. In many cases, the consequences can include expulsion or getting a zero on the exam or assignment.

It is almost impossible to recover from a zero on an exam. Professors don't take kindly to cheaters. If you have 3 exams a semester and you got a zero on one, that means 33% of your exam averages is already gone. Even if you get a 100% on each remaining exam (which you know you won't) you still get only 66% of your exam grade.

Even worse than getting a zero on an exam is expulsion. For a student who has been expelled for cheating it is almost impossible to find another school that will accept him or her. Expulsion for academic dishonesty is a stigma that stays

How Professors Prevent Cheating

- **Using multiple versions of the same exam with just slight variations of the same questions**
- **Increasing the number of exam proctors**
- **Looking for students who make the same exact errors in the same section of exams, quizzes, labs, or homework assignments.**

Are you still curious about cheating? Believe it or not, there is a book written on the topic.

The Cheater's Handbook
Bob Corbett
Regan Books; ISBN: 0060988126

The author himself sums up the book best, "...Now, though, unfortunately, he [the author] has to resort to writing books like this to make money. In other words, he [the author] doesn't recommend following his path. Study!"

with you for life!

YOUR ACADEMIC ADVISOR

In an ideal world, academic advisors are supposed to be professors who guide you through the academic process and advise you about adding or dropping a class. They're supposed to make sure you are aware of the effect of the decision(s) you make. Their signature on your add/drop form is necessary to drop a troublesome class. Finally, they're supposed to quote college rules and regulations.

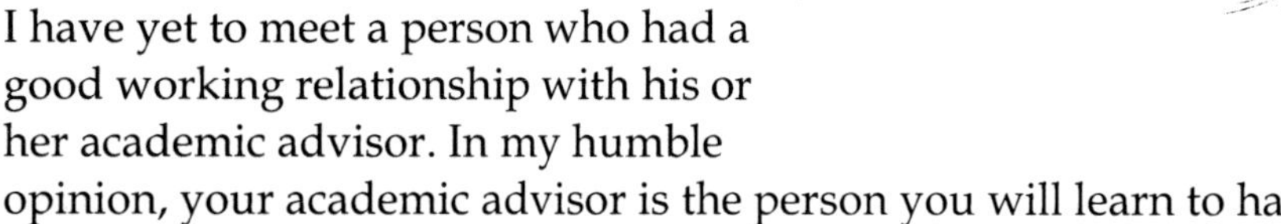

I have yet to meet a person who had a good working relationship with his or her academic advisor. In my humble opinion, your academic advisor is the person you will learn to hate.

First, take anything an advisor says with a grain of salt, but listen attentively when he or she quotes you college policies and guidelines. These are topics an advisor knows something about.

Second, always get another opinion on anything the advisor tells you. If the advice doesn't feel right, also talk to a professor you trust. There may have been students in similar situations, who have beaten the system. Besides, the second professor might be willing to help bend the rules a bit for you.

My so-called advisor, a dope *extraordinaire*, caused me to spend two summer sessions at college to catch up in my courses. Had I gone to the professors who taught the courses I needed, I would have learned that I could have taken the courses in the fall. My friends spoke to their professors, and I spent the summer session by myself.

Never assume that your conversations with your professors or your academic advisor are confidential. I remember one incident, in which I really could have used some solid advice. A class called Electronic Devices and Circuits was giving me considerable grief. I took the class during a summer session (my first mistake!) and I couldn't absorb the material fast enough for my professor. We had an exam every other week and I failed each and every one of them! I knew it was time for me to bail out before I got another F on my student transcript.

I went to my academic advisor with my trusty add/drop form in hand. After explaining why I felt it necessary to drop the class, my advisor told me, "Have you considered that you might not have what it takes to become an engineer? In fact, with your grades nobody will ever hire you. You might want to consider doing something else." Those were not the words of advice and encouragement I had expected. I could feel my self-confidence drifting away. Fortunately, I eventually shrugged off everything he had said, got my diploma, and found a well-paying job-as an engineer, no less!-just to spite him!

This incident left a very bad taste in my mouth. What I didn't know at the time was that my Electronic Devices and Circuits professor and my academic advisor were good friends. They played racquetball together after lunch and they had discussed me in detail. My advisor's "advice" was their plan for getting rid of me! Luckily I am thick-skinned and very stubborn (I hate to give up when presented with a challenge)!

The professor who gave me the best advice during my college career was outside my major. In fact, she was a literary professor. Through her travels and studies she knew more about life than most of the professors in my chosen major. She knew how to put things in perspective and taught me not to take crap from people and to strive for what I want.

SUMMER SESSIONS

As if you hadn't had enough work during the fall and spring semesters, you could take summer classes. Summer sessions are often used for one of two reasons: to get ahead or to catch up. Getting ahead means you plan to co-op or do a semester in industry during the fall. Catching up means you failed a few classes and want to graduate on time. Avoid taking a class during the summer if it is your first time for that particular class. The pace is ridiculous and the classes are long. The school tries

to cram a semester's worth of work in a little over a month. Most people can't absorb information this fast! Trust me, I know this from experience. I spent two summer sessions at my college, during which time I got very little sleep and nearly failed my classes. Technical subjects such as math, science, or certain business courses should not be taken under these conditions!

CHAPTER 9
SHOULD I JOIN A GREEK ORGANIZATION?

WHAT IS A GREEK ORGANIZATION?

Fraternities and sororities make up what is known as the Greek system. A fraternity (from Latin *frater* = brother) is a brotherhood organization comprised only of, you guessed it, male students, while a sorority (from Latin *soror* = sister) is a sisterhood organization. Fraternities and sororities often have ties to larger, national organizations, with which they share their names. These names are composed entirely of letters of the Greek alphabet, e.g., Lambda Lambda Lambda, Omega Mu Mu, Alpha Alpha Beta, or Omega Mu. Most campus Greek organizations have social mixers, compete in intramural sports, participate in charities, and perform community service.

At some colleges, as much as 30 percent of the student body claims membership in Greek organizations. Many fraternities and sororities have their own houses and members may live there instead of in dormitories or off-campus apartments. These houses are fairly large and can accommodate 30 or more brothers or sisters.

Unlike campus dormitories, Greek houses are not guaranteed to be structurally sound. One sorority house was in such need of repairs that it was condemned. Even more frightening was a certain fraternity house that burnt to the ground under suspicious circumstances.

On the other had not every Greek house is a catastrophe waiting to happen. Some of these buildings have long and proud histories. In fact one fraternity house I visited had a secret tunnel that was part of the Underground Railroad! Many Greek houses employ cooks and housekeepers. A lot of houses also have mascots, usually dogs.

The condition of a Greek house often corresponds to the reputation of the organization inhabiting it. All fraternities and sororities have their own type of notoriety on campus. One fraternity might house all the party animals. A sorority might be known for catering to ditzes. However, some Greek organizations are gathering places for

serious students. Ask around campus to find out which organization is which. Not all Greek organizations are drinking groups!

One fraternity really sticks out in my mind. Every Friday at the stroke of noon, its members tipped back ice-cold beers and played billiards on the front lawn. They seemed to be having a grand ole time, but I can't help wondering what their GPA must have looked like!

WHAT ARE THE ADVANTAGES OF JOINING?

As a member of a Greek organization you instantly have a ton of new friends so you won't lack people to hang out with. Your social calendar fills up with mixers and parties. There are opportunities to perform community service. You can make valuable alumni contacts, because Greek organizations often encourage networking with your brothers or sisters once you leave college. Some organizations publish alumni newsletters and hold alumni events so that members can schmooze their way to job opportunities. Last but not least, you will have access to fraternity/sorority files. Many organizations have old exams from previous members. These exams are valuable study aids.

WHAT ARE THE DISADVANTAGES OF JOINING?

As is the case with most things in life, too much of a good thing can be a bad thing. Social functions and community service tasks can eat up too much of your time. Spending virtually all your time with your Greek brothers or sisters may keep you from meeting people outside the Greek system. All Greek organizations charge dues, which can be expensive. Finally, there is always politics and you may find yourself as the low person on the totem pole.

WHAT SHOULD YOU KNOW BEFORE JOINING

Before you consider joining a Greek organization, you need to ask certain questions up front: What is the Greek organization about? What are its principles, ethics, and beliefs? What sort of academic assistance can it provide? Are freshman allowed leadership roles? What are the pledge requirements? How much time does the organization demand from its members?

OPINIONS ON JOINING

I took an informal poll to get some gut reactions about joining a Greek organization. One fraternity brother claimed, "There are definitely networking opportunities here-

members have all kinds of positions in the outside world." A sorority sister told me, "I am learning to organize things, by organizing our blood drive and our volleyball parties. These skills will look good on my resume." However, one fraternity brother wasn't so optimistic, "The fraternity costs me money. I pay a fee to both the local and national chapters. On top of that I have to pay dues." He also added, "If you decide that you no longer want to be a member, you may find yourself ostracized by the other members."

MY OPINION ON JOINING

There is the part where I get to be a little reflective. If I had to do it all over again, would I join a fraternity? The short answer is: Yes. Here is my long answer:

It is true that rushing (the frat word for "being recruited") a fraternity places significant demands on your time. These demands almost inevitably result in your grades dropping. Greek organizations also have been known to suppress individuality. After all, each and every one of the brothers and sisters owns the same cap and jacket. This isn't ideal, if you like to be a leader rather than a follower.

In hindsight however, my main reason for joining would be to develop better social skills. After college I soon realized that my social skills were not quite what I wanted them to be. I was never exactly what you would call the life of the party. The cutest girls were in sororities and I wouldn't have minded being in mixers with them. Having some alumni to help me get a job after college would also have been very beneficial. Lastly, I've always wanted to give someone the secret fraternity handshake.

HOW DO I JOIN A GREEK ORGANIZATION?

To attract new members, the fraternities and sororities on my campus had informal parties, which were called "smokers." Why the name is beyond me. However, at these parties you could find food, games, and friendly people to tell you how great Greek life is. A senior frat member described his house's parties: "The whole idea of frat parties is to recruit new members. Freshmen can't join in the first semester. What you do is invite them to a party, have lots of alcohol, and have lots of members there to show them you're all friends and having a good time together (even if you're not). Invite lots of women. Invite more women than guys."

The procedure for joining a Greek fraternity or sorority varies from one group to the

next. Typically you need to be invited to join. During recruitment—the "rush"—bids are handed out. Before you can become a full-fledged member, you must become what is called a pledge. Pledges are often required to perform various activities for the organization. During this period organizations tend to place the greatest demand on your time. This brings us to the issue of hazing. Hazing is illegal in most states, and most Greek organizations frown upon it.

WHAT IS HAZING?

The term 'hazing' shall mean any conduct or method of initiation into any student organization, whether on public or private property, which willfully or recklessly endangers the physical or mental health of any student or other person. Such conduct shall include whipping, beating, branding, forced calisthenics, exposure to the weather, forced consumption of any food, liquor, beverage, drug, or other substance, or any other brutal treatment or forced physical activity which is likely to adversely affect the physical health or safety of any such student or other person, or which subjects such student or other person to extreme mental stress including extended deprivation of sleep or rest or extended isolation. (Massachusetts General Laws, Chapter 24).

If the above legalese doesn't give you a clear picture of what hazing is all about, just rent the movie "Animal House." Fast forward to the part where new members are being inducted into a rival fraternity. The scene to watch is the one where an upperclassman dressed in a ceremonial robe, paddles an almost naked pledge. The pledge repeats after each paddle, "Thank you sir, may I have another?"

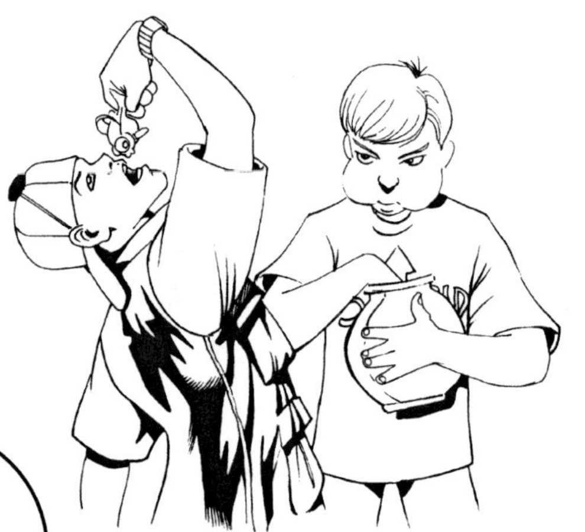

Here are some activities that can be construed as hazing:

- Conducting "Hell Week" activities (the name itself should give you a clue!), keeping the date of initiation/pre-initiation secret (thus restricting access to only those invited and banning all others), or restricting work parties to new members only (whatever happened to equality?). Requiring new members to perform certain actions, such as phone duty (this is not volunteer work-it is demanded), sit-ups (if you

get tired and want to stop, too bad), or becoming a personal slave to another member (slavery is illegal). Making someone lift heavy objects or carry things for another member can also be considered hazing.

- Keeping members from attending class, depriving them of sleep, or requiring them to practice periods of silence (this is hazing if it causes physical or mental distress!). It's also considered hazing to prevent a member from looking after their personal hygiene.
- Treating members in a unacceptable social manner; for example, requiring them to use separate entrances to the chapter house (while everybody else goes in through the main entrance) and forcing them to dress uncomfortably or inappropriately. One should not have to submit to these kinds of "torture" simply to be part of an organization.
- Applying permanent tattoos to someone (you could wind up in a court of law over this!).

CHAPTER 10
THE QUIRKS OF EVERYDAY COLLEGE LIFE

Living on campus is like living in a miniature city. There's a population (student body), police force (campus security), laws (campus regulations), government (student government and college bureaucracy), homes (dorms and on-campus apartments), media (campus TV, radio, and newspaper), culture, and even criminals (scam artists and stalkers). All these combine to form an equation that makes up your everyday campus life.

CAMPUS SERVICES

MAIL

Campus mail was a constant thorn in my side. Because much of the mailroom staff were students performing work-study, mail delivery tended to be very erratic. This was particularly true of packages that didn't fit in a mail slot.

Packages would end up in an endless void called *The Package Room*. Once I received a package slip in my mailbox I would have to trek up to The Package Room to retrieve my parcel. Unfortunately, The Package Room was never open during posted hours, so when I finally did get my care package from home the content was usually stale.

I had my share of fights with the campus mail staff. The straw that really broke the camel's back were packages sent NEXT DAY AIR. I was lucky to receive these within a week of their arrival date.

Fighting campus mail delivery is futile. Not all campuses have bad mail delivery, but mine did. The solution is to rent a mailbox for four years from the local Mailboxes USA. Trust me, you'll find this worth every penny. It also guarantees that you have a constant address for four years. Unlike a post office box, UPS and other parcel handlers will

deliver packages to a Mailbox USA address. Why deal with the bird brains who run the campus mail when, for a small fee, you can hire professionals?(!)

CAMPUS CONVENIENCE STORE

Most campuses have some type of variety store where almost every necessity of life can be purchased. However, prices at the campus convenience store, just like those at the campus bookstore, are always highly inflated. But of course, there is the convenience of not having to leave campus for such essentials as cough syrup, potato chips, and magazines.

Again, just like the campus bookstore, the campus convenience store is subject to influence by the college. Here is one typical example of the ill effect the influence of the academic institution can have on the convenience store business. Many of us students were devoutly loyal to our brand of soft drink. When a major soft drink manufacturer picked up the tab for the campus hockey arena's amazingly expensive electronic scoreboard, the campus convenience store was forbidden to sell soft drink products manufactured by our generous benefactor's competitors. So my brand became suddenly and inconveniently unavailable at the school's convenience store.

CABLE SERVICE

The Cable Company in my college town was my favorite institution to hate! Not only did it enjoy an unfair monopoly, it also practiced what I considered really unfair deeds. The company often offered free trials of premium channels such as Disney and Cinemax, but refused these promotions to students. To add insult to injury, the company also refused to pick up such stations as the Cartoon Network and the Sci-Fi Channel. The cable company was completely unsympathetic to our pleas, so my friends and I threatened to put a satellite dish on the roof and buy a receiver (after all, we were engineering students). With services such as Direct TV now readily available, fortunately there's a viable alternative to local cable service!

CAMPUS NEWSPAPER

This is where you get to find out what's happening on campus in a politically correct, antiseptic format. Lucky for me, though, my campus newspaper was under the watchful eye of a very liberal-minded professor as its advisor and it printed my movie reviews even though they were full of downright zany comments. If you ever want to become known on campus, writing for the school newspaper is an excellent forum.

The campus newspaper is the best place to send a message to everyone on campus. It's better than the bulletin boards. Vendors from the local area place ads to let students know about specials, sales, and upcoming social events. Also on Valentine's Day it could the best place to let your campus sweetheart know how you feel about her or him!

THE TRUTH ABOUT SOME CAMPUS SERVICES

THE TRUTH ABOUT CAMPUS RADIO STATION GIVEAWAYS

Have you ever wanted to win free stuff on the radio? Well, in college it's possible! College radio stations have a limited number of listeners at best. In fact, there's so much dead air time—time when nobody calls in— that during contests DJs call their friends off the air and tell them to call in and be the next caller. Poof! Free concert tickets! I saw this happen all the time, and my roommate acquired several CDs that way. My advice is to become great friends with a DJ as soon as possible.

THE TRUTH ABOUT STUDENT GOVERNMENT

Unfortunately, student government is about as bad as the one that resides in Washington DC. Student officials knuckle under to special interest groups, and bribery. My particular student government was a master at embezzlement.

Consider this cautionary tale:

I was disappointed when I learned how my student government squandered my activities fees. Instead of spending the money on organizing campus events such as movie nights, concerts, or Senior Week, our campus politicians spent the money on elaborate ski getaways for themselves.

So what is Senior Week? I am glad you asked! It is a weeklong party for graduating seniors after final exam week and before commencement. When my Senior Week finally surfaced after four long years, I found that almost no activities had been planned. The reason, of course, was the diversion of our funds to all those ski getaways. Our class officers knew enough to bail. They went home and left 800 disgruntled seniors in the dorms with nothing to do for a week! Lets just say a lynch mob formed and was looking for the class president.

On graduation day I finally saw my class president. The speech he gave was as embarrassing as his money management skills. I felt angry for not taking a more active role in student government and throwing the bum out. Like any government, student government is only as responsible as its constituents are vigilant. LEARN FROM THIS TALE!

DORM-LIFE SNAFUS

LOCKUPS

One of my biggest complaints about dorm life was about dorm lockups. During breaks and vacations, security would lock up the dormitories on Friday evening before vacation and students were locked out of the dorms until break was over. During one vacation my ride was late and I couldn't leave until Saturday morning. I explained my plight to campus security to no avail. I was told to find somewhere else to stay, which isn't easy when home is an eight-hour drive away. Naturally, I disobeyed and stayed in the dorm anyway. I really didn't have a choice, because the temperature was below freezing and it was snowing! I stayed in my room, but had to leave the dorm to get dinner. All the cafeterias were closed. Fortunately a friend was able to let me back into the building. For his good deed, however, he was severely reprimanded by campus security. He was told, "If you let one more person back into this dorm, I'm putting you out in the cold."

The response I got from the Dean of Campus Housing was even worse, "I don't care where you stay, but you are not staying in the dorms. Find someplace else to sleep tonight." I must say I felt better knowing that my tuition helped pay that bastard's salary. I am certain there is a section of hell reserved for him.

THE HOUSING LOTTERY

On every campus, some living quarters are more desirable than others. On my campus there was a set of dorms that were especially desirable. These were the townhouse dorms-two-bedroom apartments, each with a full kitchen, bathroom, and shower. There were only two ways to get one of these choice assignments—by squatting or by lucking out in the house lottery.

Squatting meant that an upperclassman, usually a junior, who already lived there, could extend occupancy for the next year, rendering it unavailable to newcomers. The housing lottery might as well have been a game show called "You Can't Win." All students were given a lottery number. The lower your number the better. Housing was assigned by year, then by lottery number amongst those of the same year. Juniors picked what was left over after seniors had chosen; sophomores picked from what juniors didn't choose, and so on. If you got a high lottery number you were screwed. For three years in a row most of my friends got high lottery numbers and didn't get the housing they wanted.

FINDING PLACES TO STUDY

Often your dorm room is not the best place to study. Your roommate might have his or her significant other over. Somebody down the hall might be blasting a stereo. You might wait up till everyone is asleep, only to have to listen to your roommate snoring. This can be very distracting.

Ultimately, you need a quality place to study. Study lounges and the library tend to get crowded around exam time, and finding an empty table and chair can be difficult. The worst part about the library is that no food is allowed inside. So you can't bring your favorite caffeine-enhanced beverage to keep you awake during long study sessions. Now that I have eliminated all of the obvious places, let me reveal the best-kept secrets as far as study places are concerned:

- Empty Class Rooms—On my campus many buildings were still open after classes had finished for the day. I would walk into an empty classroom, snap on the lights, and close the door. Nobody bothered me, and peace and quiet were abundant.
- Food Court—I found that the food court on my campus was open until late hours. You could grab a table and spread out your books. It wasn't as quiet as an empty classroom, but it was convenient (especially if I got a case of the munchies).
- Empty Rooms in the Student Union—At night, many rooms in the student union were fairly inactive. I grabbed an empty office, turned on the light, spread out my books, and closed the doors. This place also proved to be convenient since it was near the campus convenience store where I could buy ample quantities of popcorn and caffeine-rich soda!

CRAZINESS - STRESS RELIEF

You're at college. Spontaneous bursts of craziness can occur whenever stress escalates beyond tolerable levels. The human mind can tolerate only so much before it needs an outlet. Sometimes the usual pranks and water fights just won't do.

During one final exam week, my cohorts and I invented a game, which we called "Head Chopper," the ultimate form of hallway Frisbee. The object of the game was to throw a Frisbee with as much spin and force as possible at the person(s) at the other end of the hallway. When our RA had disappeared to the study lounge we played a half-hour round with six Frisbees. We broke the exit sign and knocked out two ceiling tiles. I ended up destroying a pair of eyeglasses-the result of a Frisbee hit to the face. I considered it my badge of courage. (Think of the sequence in the movie "Tron" involving the deadly disks.)

At a very famous high-stress college populated by world-renowned geniuses, the students were far more destructive than we ordinary mortals at my college could have imagined! These Einsteins cleared everybody off the dormitory grounds, then dropped a piano from the top story window!

Fortunately, I was slightly less destructive. One day, when nobody was looking, I roller-bladed on the brand new linoleum floors of the student union. Of course this was

strictly *verboten*!

For me, the best stress relief in college was the "Rocky Horror Picture Show," a cult movie that played at midnight at the local theater. Audience participation was encouraged, and people came dressed like characters in the movie! On cue audience members threw rice, toast, and toilet paper! It was all harmless fun. I remember returning to the dorm at around 2:00 a.m. picking rice out of my hair. More importantly, all my stress was gone!

Before I learned how to manage my stress my roommate nicknamed me "BOS," or "BOSman" (short for Ball of Stress). I got so stressed that my face would break out, and I couldn't eat. The bottom line is: sometimes you've got to blow off a little steam or you'll spontaneously combust. (For the record, I do not advocate shooting Frisbees at exit signs, roller-blading on linoleum floors, or throwing pianos out of windows. Instead I recommend trying something less destructive!)

TOWN VS. GOWN

Depending on your college's location, the primary reason for your college town's existence might be the college itself. That was definitely true for my college town. It had two purposes: To exploit students and to provide the worst possible service in return. Prices were exorbitant and merchants rarely went out of their way to be helpful. They knew that they had us in a bind, because the nearest mall was 22 miles away!

GETTING A HAIR CUT

Beware of hair stylists. Some have no style at all! If your college is not in a metropolis but out in the sticks, your choice is limited. Your hair clipper may work more like a hedge trimmer. Recalling some of the hatchet jobs I have received is still very painful. On graduation day my hair looked like I had lost a fight with a pair of lawn mowers! Ask around before getting a haircut. Find out which salons have a bad reputation. Fortunately, in my town we had a barber named Buzz. He was reasonably priced and well liked by most of the college guys but he cut hair like a buzz saw. There just wasn't a single stylist in the entire town who could groom my hair in the high quality manner to which I was accustomed.

TOWNIES

Townies, the indigenous population of your college town, can be an experience! Because my town was in a rural area, there were significant cultural differences between us students and our townie counterparts. It seemed that most young townies wore combat fatigues, drove hot rods or large trucks, and viewed us with utter contempt.

SCAMS AND RIP-OFFS

Every salesman in the world knows that college freshmen have money in their pockets. You and your classmates will have scholarship money and cash gifts that you received at your high school graduation party. Freshman year will be the only year that you ever have money to spare. These salesmen will do everything in their power to relieve you of that cash. Here are some of the more unscrupulous tactics I have seen.

SWEEPSTAKES

My favorite scam directed at college students is the infamous, "You won a sweepstakes!" trick. Every student on campus receives a yellow postcard that reads: "You [insert your name here], have just won the XXX Sweepstakes and Giveaway." The prizes include a brand-new car, a few thousand in cash, a VCR, and last but not least, a $500 coupon book. As indicated on the card, you are supposed to believe you have definitely won one of these prizes. They all sound pretty good, right? You may be wondering about that coupon book. Okay, that one doesn't sound as appealing as the others. But as long as you don't win that one, who cares! Right? WRONG!

To claim your prize you have to dial a 1-900 number. No problem. The most that could cost is $2.00 a minute. Wait, this one costs $30! Why would you have to pay $30 to collect a prize you already won? If you go ahead and make the call, you'll be notified that you won the coupon book. Guess what, you just paid $30 for a coupon book! Flip over the postcard and look at the odds of winning the coupon book: you'll find they are 1 to 1! Congratulations sucker, you just bought a book of worthless coupons.

RADIO STATION GIVEAWAY

Believe it or not, some scams are more elaborate than the one above! Imagine the following clever little plot designed to separate you from your money. The phone rings. You get a pre-recorded message from some radio station you've never heard of telling you to call back in five minutes for the grand prize. They give you an 800 number. You dial the

number, and five minutes later you are informed that the call will cost $50! HANG UP! You've been scammed!

BOGUS BILLS

This last scam is probably the most insidious! You receive E-mail from some obscure company claiming that you're delinquent on a bill and that unless you pay immediately you will be subject to legal action. The sender gives you a phone number to call. The number looks like a US number, but wait, in reality it's in the Bahamas! The cost of the call is $50 a minute! The real killer is that you don't actually get to talk to that person ("Call later ... unavailable"). If you're crazy enough to try again, you'll get billed another $50!

SCHOOL CULTURE

One item not covered in the brochure about your college is its traditions and rivalries. My college had an on-going rivalry with the State College down the road. This rivalry got magnified every year during the first major snowstorm. The students from the state school would come over the bridge and attack The Pit with snowballs. Of course, we had to go outside and defend our college's honor! One year the battle got way out of hand. The students from state rolled a twelve-foot snowball in front of our dorm. It took a tractor to remove it!

CHAPTER 11
PRANKS AND HIJINKS

THE PRANKSTER

College wouldn't be any fun without the mischief and mayhem that occurs when nobody is looking. For many of you, college is your first time away from home. It's your first chance to test the boundaries of authority. When the hours get late and the RA isn't around, the craziness starts! Remember pranks break up the tedium of the daily grind. Expect the unexpected!

Living in a cold environment where you can play outside only a few months out of the year took its toll on me and my fellow dormmates. Cabin fever set in early. Since I and my fellow doormmates were freshmen, we not only thought we were indestructible, but breaking new ground in mischief. Looking back on the experience now, I can honestly say I don't believe we were real trailblazers. I am providing the following descriptions of various pranks, not to inspire you but to make you more difficult prey to tricksters.

DORM ROOM DOOR PRANKS

PENNIES IN THE DOOR JAM

Beyond any shadow of a doubt the most dangerous and annoying prank is the pennies-in-the-dorm-jam stunt. I won't go into the details of how it's done because I'd hate to see it done to somebody else. The scenario is that some bozo wedges pennies into your dorm jam. This makes it impossible to open the door. Once this happens you are stuck in the room. To avoid this trap, when you first arrive at your dorm, pop the door pins halfway up out of their hinges. Once loosened, they'll be easier to remove. If you find yourself penny'ed in, pop the pins out of the hinges and unhook the door from the frame. Voilà, instant freedom!

During my freshman year this stunt was very common. One group of pranksters

penny'ed in my RA, and the head resident had to use a hammer and crowbar to get him out of his room. I was once penny'ed into a windowless bathroom for three hours. Three guys, a hammer, and a crowbar were necessary to get me out!

BUCKET OF WATER

Another prank involving a door is the old bucket-of-water trick. Since most residence hall doors open into the room, if a person leans an object against the door when it's opened, the object will fall into the room. This is particularly worrisome if the object in question is a trash barrel filled with ten gallons of water. The damage that can be caused by this is tremendous. I watched in horror as this stunt was performed on my next-door neighbor. Unfortunately, he had left his computer on the floor and found himself watching as it was engulfed by a tidal wave of water. The moral of the story is: NEVER open your door without looking through the peephole first.

ELECTRICAL APPLIANCE FIASCOES

Electrical appliances are a prankster's playground. Your microwave, refrigerator, and alarm clock are all fertile ground for the relentless prankster to plant some havoc in your life.

MICROWAVE MADNESS

One favorite trick is to toss an egg into the microwave, press START, and then run. After the egg heats up it will explode and make a royal mess inside the microwave. Another stunt that could end up damaging the microwave is to place a compact disk in it and press START. Not only will sparks be generated, but the disk will be rendered permanently unplayable. If you own a microwave beware of these thrill seekers.

REFRIGERATOR EXPLOSIONS

Refrigerators are usually subjected to one stunt in particular—soda can explosions. A prankster places a can of soda or beer into the freezer compartment. Once the liquid freezes it expands and bursts through the can. This creates a mess that will require you to defrost the freezer compartment to clean it up.

ALARM CLOCK HORROR

The last electrical appliance stunt isn't as messy but just as annoying. The scenario is as follows. Some jerk comes into your room and changes the time on your alarm clock. You, the target of the joke, end up being really early or really late for your next class.

BEDTIME NIGHTMARES

In addition to worrying about your electrical appliances you might want to consider sleeping with one eye open. Besides the typical short-sheet incident, your bed may be subjected to such nasty items as water balloons and plungers. Pranksters will often stuff water balloons into your bed, mattress and pillowcase. When you crawl into bed, you get

soaked. Another trick is to stuff things into bed with you while you're sleeping. One person I knew had a morbid fear of plungers. Pranksters stuffed a plunger in bed with him one night so that they could watch him freak out the next morning! Another variation of the same trick is to toss a vacuum cleaner under the covers while someone is sleeping. Once the normally harmless household appliance is in place, some jerk turns it on and watches the victim's reaction to get a cheap thrill.

DORM ROOM STUNTS

ROOM CLEANOUTS

Always lock your room when you and your roommate are out. On my campus, whenever somebody left a room unlocked one particular prankster would be on the prowl. His favorite stunt was to enlist several of his henchmen and empty the entire dorm-room contents into a bathroom, then reassemble it. This eye for detail enhanced the prank's effectiveness.

The prankster would then call a resident of the room he had just emptied, asking to borrow some item that would require the resident to return to his room. The poor victim would come back to find it completely empty. Several people standing nearby with smirks on their faces would point to the bathroom, where the prankster and his henchman were waiting with a camera to capture the poor guy's expression on finding all his furniture rearranged between urinals and shower stalls.

ROOM STUFFING

Room cleanouts are not the only prank to which your room could be subjected while you and your roommate(s) are out. Another favorite trick that pranksters love is to stuff your room full of trash and other junk. Even when your door is locked, people can still toss stuff into your room. The opening between your door and the floor is just wide enough for popcorn, Styrofoam peanuts, and Cheerios to slide through. To speed up the process, someone can use a hair dryer to blow these and other interesting objects under the door.

BATHROOM CRAZINESS

SHOWER STUNTS

Your room is not the only place in the dormitory pranksters like to target. The bathroom is a playground for all kinds of tricks. Showering in a freshman dorm can be an adventure. For example, a joker on my floor used to throw buckets of cold water at people in the shower. Another used to take my bathrobe and towels and move them outside the bathroom. Fortunately, there were no girls on my floor when I went to retrieve them. Moral: Always keep an eye on your stuff!

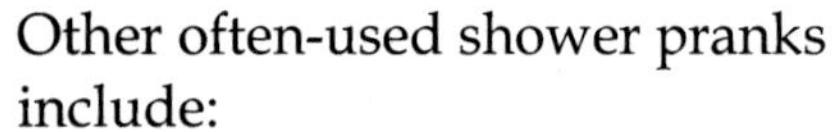

Other often-used shower pranks include:

- Throwing flour into the shower. (Adding water turns it gluey so that it sticks to you.)
- Throwing Kool-Aid into the shower. (This turns you bright red or blue or whatever color the prankster uses.)
- Turning off the hot water while you're showering. (There's nothing like suddenly finding yourself showering in ice cold water!)

One morning I experienced the ultimate bizarre shower prank. I woke up and headed to the shower as usual. However, this particular morning I found a large brown item in an empty shower stall next to me. Upon closer inspection, I realized it was a coyote! The night before, a bunch of guys went out hunting and shot a coyote. They skinned it and were using the shower stall to cure the pelt. Not only did it startle me to find a dead animal in the shower, it freaked my hallmates out as well.

MISCELLANEOUS BATHROOM HIJINKS

A shower stall is not the only place in the bathroom where you're at the mercy of pranksters. Watch out for the following:

- Black shoe polish on toilet seats.
- Party snappers under toilet seats (these innocuous little noise makers can cause quite a commotion and startle people).

The last (but not the least) prank to worry about in a freshman bathroom is the hot flash. Quite often the plumbing in your dormitory will be very primitive. The university or college found the contractor who gave the lowest possible bid to construct it. As a result, it may have its share of quirks. In my case, this meant whenever somebody flushed a toilet, cold water stopped running in the showers and people taking showers got scolded with hot water. Sometimes to be cruel, pranksters would randomly flush toilets while people were in the showers.

FIRE ALARMS

Freshman dorms have an unusually large number of fire alarms. Many of them end up being false alarms. Typically, some idiot gets drunk and grabs the alarm lever while trying to get up off the floor. Sometimes a prankster from another dorm decides you and your neighbors are getting too much sleep and should be awakened at 3:30 a.m.

No matter what, fire alarms always get pulled at the most inconvenient times, usually while you're asleep. The worst incidents occur when you get caught in the shower. I saw a guy wrapped in a towel with shampoo in his hair standing outside in zero degree weather because he was caught by a fire alarm. Very rarely do you get to find the jerk who pulled the alarm. Keep in mind that pulling a fire alarm is a criminal offense. Also there is no way of knowing which fire alarms are real and which are false. Therefore you must treat each alarm as the real thing.

During final exam week, you might find smoke detectors in various dorm rooms going off. Again, this is the work of a prankster. Since final exam week typically features 24-hour quiet hours, making noise is a task that pranksters delight in. A prankster will call your room claiming to be campus safety performing a routine test of the smoke detectors. You'll be asked to press the test button on your room's smoke detector. If you comply, you'll have become an unwilling accomplice in violating quiet hours.

MAIL BOMBS

Your campus mailbox is also subject to pranksters. Beware of mail bombs! A mail bomb has nothing to do with sending explosive devices in the mail. Nor does it have anything to do with the Unabomber. However, being the recipient of a mail bomb can be very annoying. My senior-year roommate was one such recipient. Each day he opened his mailbox to find dozens of catalogs, free samples, coupons, and other assorted junk that he had not ordered. As the days went by, the incoming mail got weirder and weirder. Someone had filled out a bunch of reader request cards from different

magazines using my roommate's name and campus address!

TELEPHONES

In addition to worrying about your campus mailbox, realize that your telephone is also fair game to pranksters. If your campus has call forwarding for your phone service, don't be surprised if you suddenly find that your phone stops ringing. What typically happens is that some trickster sneaks into your room when you're not looking, picks up your phone, and enables call forwarding, sending your phone calls elsewhere. Sometimes your phone will go completely dead. Some trickster has found the junction box with the connections for your dormitory and has shorted out your phone line!

The last phone prank you have to worry about can end up costing you money. If your long-distance company uses a PIN number (personal identification number), make sure you don't inadvertently give it out by leaving it in plain view! After I graduated and headed home, I received a $1000 phone bill for calls made to China! Not only do I not know anybody in China, but I didn't make the calls! Somebody obtained my PIN! Fortunately, I was able to prove that I didn't make the calls and didn't have to pay for them.

MISCELLANEOUS STUNTS

I don't have a category for this next set of stunts. However, each prank involved me. I was either the culprit or on the receiving end:

- The Birthday Incident — Every year I dreaded the approach of my birthday. My roommates and friends always took the occasion as an excuse to add a little bit of craziness to my life. Often the pranks just involved throwing surprise parties for me and getting me gag gifts. However, during my senior year my friends, the pranksters, pulled out all the stops. On the night of my 22nd birthday, I found a guy standing in front of my door, wearing a dress and lipstick. He sang me a seductive version of "Happy Birthday" Marilyn Monroe style! My jaw dropped to the floor! Before I could recover from the shock, my friends had already grabbed snapshots of my surprised expression!
- The Tuna Fish Caper — I once spent a summer session at college with a roommate who never stopped pulling practical jokes on me. One day I couldn't take being on the receiving end of his gags any longer. He needed to be taught a lesson. He was a compulsive tuna-fish eater, so I bought a can of tuna fish cat food. I removed the

label from a can of tuna fish intended for people and glued it onto the cat food can, then placed the cat food with my roommate's supply of tuna fish. Imagine his surprise when he opened the

❑ can and noticed that his tuna fish was bright red!

FACULTY AND CAMPUS REGIME VICTIMS

Students aren't the only ones subjected to practical jokes. Sometimes professors, too, are caught by them! One professor who was thoroughly disliked by the entire student body decided to demonstrate a pulley system to his physics class. He invited students to lift him up, using the pulley. One student lifted the professor almost to the ceiling, then tied the pulley rope to a support beam—and walked away! The professor was stuck, suspended in mid air. A janitor had to let him down. In another case, the entire campus bureaucracy was the target of a fraternity prank. A fraternity managed to put its dog through four years of college and earn a bachelor's degree! In fact, the dog's name was called on graduation day!

CHAPTER 12
LAUNDRY

Laundry is one of the lows of college life. You've been given all this freedom, however, at laundry time it's time to pay the piper. That's when responsibility keeps knocking at the door. Avoid doing laundry as long as possible! It is my belief that you shouldn't have to do laundry more than every two weeks. But if you're one of those students who lives close to home, by all means take it home every weekend!

When doing laundry always have lots of quarters. The last thing you need is to run out of change! Find out ahead of time how much it costs to do a load in the washer and dryer. Many campuses allow students to use debit cards for laundry, in which case, make sure you have ample credit.

Before even attempting to do laundry, find out when is the best time. Remember that everybody else in your dorm has to use the same set of machines. There are going to be times when the laundry room gets really busy. Often the best time to do laundry is late at night and in the wee hours of the morning. Avoid weekends. Everybody does laundry on weekends. If a break or vacation is coming up, take the laundry home; don't bother giving the school any more of your money.

To do laundry, you will need to invest some time. It takes almost half an hour for the washing cycle and another 45 minutes for the drying cycle. So figure about one and a half hours to do a load. Never leave clothes in the machines! People will remove them when they need a machine. You could lose clothes that way! Sometimes people even put your clothes on the floor and get them dirty again! (This happened to me!)

When you are ready to use the washing machine, put whites with whites and set the knob to the position marked WHITES. Put colors in a separate load. This simple rule of thumb, however, does not apply to certain delicate pieces of clothing. But you should not bring clothing to college that requires special care, anyway! Set the knob to PERMANENT PRESS. DO NOT MIX LOADS. Never overstuff the washing machine. One frugal student decided to put all his laundry in one load. He started the permanent press cycle and walked away. A few

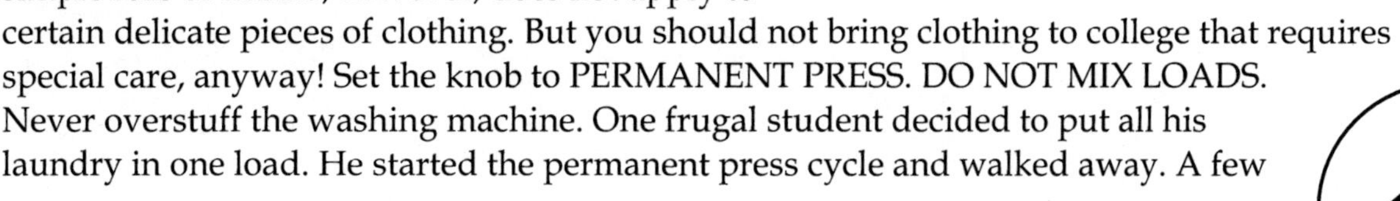

minutes later the machine began to buck and bolt like a bronco! His clothes were covered in smoke! The smell was horrendous.

When choosing a washing machine, keep in mind that these machines have been used and abused. Determine which machines are running better than others. I remember one washing machine that was so off balance that I had to sit on top of it to get my load finished.

Before you use a dryer, always open it up and remove the lint from the lint guard. Otherwise you're going to spend significant time removing lint from your clothes! Spread out the load. Jeans take the longest time to dry. Never put more than two pairs of jeans in a single load in a dryer. Use multiple dryers with small loads in order to have your clothes dry quicker. If you end up putting larger loads into a single dryer, you may need more then one 45-minute cycle to get everything dry.

Fold T-shirts, socks, and underwear as soon as they come out of the dryer, then place them into your laundry basket. Take pants, and put them on a hanger immediately. Do the same with button shirts. This way you won't have to iron your clothes.

As for detergents, I recommend using a liquid because liquids are easier to measure than powders (you just fill the cap). Also liquids come concentrated, so you can do more loads with less detergent.

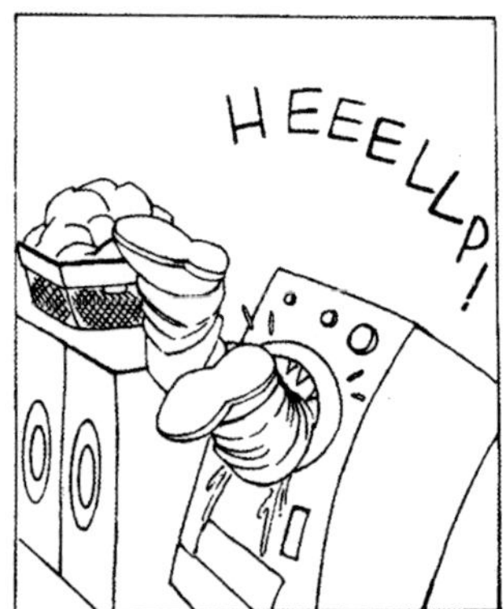

CHAPTER 13
ARRIVAL

One warm summer day in late August my parents and I arrived at my college campus. The seemingly endless summer of my senior year of high school finally came to an end. Our car was filled with all my worldly possessions—clothes, TV, stereo, and all kinds of stuff. My pockets were lined with the money I had received at my high school graduation party. It was as though an invisible sign that read "COLLEGE FRESHMAN" hung above my head.

Fortunately, there were others like me. Misery loves company. I could see a hundred or so other cars with students and parents as we pulled up to my dorm. We exchanged nervous glances as we passed by. In addition to cramped legs, I had enormous butterflies in my stomach.

I soon found myself in a large, de-iced hockey arena where I and 700 other freshman went to pick up our school-provided computers. As I looked around, familiarizing myself with the faces of the people with whom I would spend the next four years of my life, my father shared his thoughts with me: "You've got an amazing opportunity here that I never had. I wish I were going with you."

My guess is that your arrival won't be all that different from mine. In this chapter I hope to be able to prevent some of the uneasiness that I endured during my first few days of campus living. Remember, everybody surrounding you is no better off than you are.

After arriving at your dorm, the first thing you'll want to do is pick up your room key. There's no sense lugging all your belongings inside the building if you can't get into your room. Usually somebody from the housing staff or one of the RAs dispenses keys. You'll probably pick up your mailbox key at the same time.

I also received what was referred to as a "Good Stuff" box, full of goodies. These so-called goodies consisted of free samples and coupons such as:

- A small vile of Nyquil
- Two Tylenol tablets
- A small cologne/perfume sample
- A travel-size can of Edge Gel shaving cream
- Lots of miscellaneous coupons

- ❑ A disposable razor
- ❑ Candy
- ❑ Cosmetics (for female students)

Often, but not always, colleges have ambassadors of good will who will help you move in. On my campus these kindhearted people were called SOS—upperclassmen. They had volunteered their time to come back to school early to help incoming freshmen move in. It was great having a second set of hands to lift heavy objects up three flights of stairs.

Arriving at my room before my roommate gave me a few advantages. First, it allowed me to choose which side of the room I wanted. Second, it gave me the opportunity to take my pick of the furniture. (I promptly grabbed the better of the two chairs.) Third, I was able to move my stuff in without having to worry about walking over his.

Once I was settled in I began exploring. I walked down the floor, passing all the rooms. This gave me an opportunity to check out who my neighbors were. If someone looked like he needed help moving in, I offered it. This gave me a chance to introduce myself and meet my hallmates.

By the time evening rolled around, most of the students had arrived. My RA held a floor meeting, told us that his name was Dave, explained the rules, and made us introduce ourselves. He told us about all the activities that we could plan and encouraged our suggestions. He finished by saying that his door would always be open to us. He ended up being the best RA I ever had.

During your first few weeks of dorm living, I encourage you to leave your door partially open when you are home and awake. This gives people a chance to stop by and introduce themselves. You'll find that you'll make friends quickly. If you and your roommate are compatible, you'll already have made one friend. The best way to get to know people is to participate in dorm events, such as softball games, Frisbee, Jell-O snarfing contests, and canoe races.

Once you've settled into your room, you'll probably want to explore the campus and surrounding town. It's in your best interest to learn your way around campus as soon as possible. This way you won't have to spend your first few days desperately searching for your classrooms. It will also give you a chance to find out where the hangouts are, such as the student union and the gym.

SAFETY AT NIGHT

While you are out exploring, be careful at night. I recommend that girls stay in well-lit areas and avoid walking alone for extended periods of time. On my campus there were many alleged stalkings of female students. At least once a month there was a new police composite sketch of some guy who attempted a stalking. I'm not trying to scare anybody, but remember there are wackos and sickos no matter where you go. Whenever possible tell roommates and friends where you're going.

MAKING FRIENDS AND SOCIALIZING

Once you have settled into your dormitory life there is one problem you may encounter if you do not live on a coed floor or in a coed dormitory: It may be difficult to make friends with fellow students of the opposite sex. As a coed, who lived on an all-girls' floor told me, "A lot of girls who lived on coed floors got to make friends with the guys on the same floor. But I met most of my guy friends either randomly or by being introduced through other girls who had guy friends on their floors. My closest guy friend lived on the other side of campus in a roach-infested apartment."

My situation was not all that different, since I lived in an all-guy dorm during my freshman year. There were six floors of nothing but guys! Whenever a girl walked on my floor, everybody opened his door to get a glance (girls were not a common sight on my floor). Sometimes girls would eat in our cafeteria. It was commonly believed by us guys that the girls were window-shopping.

To solve the above problem, you'll have to take some initiative. The guys in my dorm did just that and decided to hold a dance in our cafeteria. They had a contest to see which floor could get the most girls to attend. All the guys put in a tremendous effort. At the end of the night a total of ten girls showed up. No enough to go around, but at least the guys had made an effort to socialize.

On the flipside, the girls in the all-girl dorm also took some initiative. They walked down to our dorm and wrote their names on the message boards on our doors. This became even more interesting when a group of girls from the state school down the road also joined in the fun, leaving a series of thought-provoking messages on every door on our floor.

One year, I again lived in a dorm that was almost entirely male. An RA arranged a social mixer between the guys and the inhabitants of the freshmen women's dorm. The mixer was set up as a combination canoe trip and picnic. Unfortunately, as we canoed to our destination picnic grounds, the girls went one way and the guys went another. As the old saying goes, "You can lead a horse to water, but you can't make him drink." Nobody took any initiative. The moral of this story is: Take advantage of opportunities handed to you!

CONCLUSION

Now that you have read my book, I hope that I have given you a taste of what the college experience is all about and that you will no longer be easy prey to the pratfalls of college. Try to learn from my mistakes and emulate my successes, if you are so inclined.

MISSED OPPORTUNITIES

While I studied like mad to get my degree, I forgot about my social life and my hobbies. Like many of my peers, I neglected to date or meet new people. I didn't even spend much time hanging out with friends. Dating after college, I discovered, gets even harder. Meeting that special someone is never easy if you don't start practicing early.

My hobbies deteriorated during my college years into watching movies and television. I gave up my inclination of becoming a classical pianist (or, at the very least, a good honky tonk player). Sadly, I also stopped reading just for fun.

No doubt, the greatest missed opportunity was the road not taken. I didn't realize then that I should have taken more classes outside my major. A class in marketing or business, for instance, would have helped my career as an engineer tremendously. It really is a good idea to think out of that proverbial box.

ADVICE

Indulge me while I climb on my soapbox for a few paragraphs. If you really hated the advice I dished out in previous chapters, you probably would not be reading these lines anyway. Ok, here we go:

In spite of my laments, some professors are actually good mentors. But there are all too few of them, and if you do find one, keep in touch with that person. Maintain a good dialogue with him or her during and after college. I had one professor who was a mentor to me, and I must say, she made a difference in my life.

Don't ever let the college dictate your college experience to you. If you are not getting good value for your money, make it known. Don't think for a moment that you are at the college's mercy. Your tuition pays the salaries of everybody employed there. If you have an incompetent professor, tell somebody. Why should a moron earn $80,000 a

year?

Learn how to live with people. Become adept at living with roommates. Why? Because after college you might still need a roommate to share the rent!

Finally, find balance in your life. Aristotle's "golden mean" may strike you as humdrum and boring, but there is wisdom in it, too. Don't spend all your time studying, but don't spend all your time socializing and partying either. For a happy and fulfilled life, you need both an education and relationships.

WHAT TO DO AFTER IT IS ALL OVER

First and foremost, join a gym. Shrug that 15 pounds you put on. Pay attention to both your personal and your professional life. Make sure you have a sound mind and a sound body. Don't spend all your 24 hours in bed, in your car, and in front of your computer. Stay physically fit. Remember, you'll need your body for at least another 50 years or so.

Second, hold on to the books from your core curriculum. If you decide on graduate school, you may need some of them again. Also, you never know, once you have a job, when you might need to look up a piece of theory in one of those books.

Third, apply what you learned in practice. College gives you a ton of theory. It is entirely up to you to transform your book smarts into earning a living. Always look for new skills that you can pick up at a job. Keep updating your resume. Never become stagnant or complacent. In the real world you are only as good as your last job.

SOUR GRAPES AND REVENGE

A review of an earlier edition of this book claimed that my approach to college "seems like the dining hall was serving sour grapes." Well, on one particular day that was indeed true! On that day, after my institution of higher learning had put the screws to me for four long years, I experienced an incident that was like the straw the broke the camel's back.

It was getting close to graduation day, when 1400 parents descended upon my small college town to see their kids graduate from college. Upstate New York does not exactly have a plethora of hotel accommodations, so my parents were unable to secure a hotel room. Never missing an opportunity to make a few bucks by exploiting people under duress, my college offered a simple and (to the college) profitable solution to the parental lodging dilemma.

For $80 a night my parents could stay in a college dorm room. They would be entitled to the same leaky plumbing, and rickety furniture that had served me so well for four years. Needless to say my parents deserved much better for their hard-earned money. Not only did the school profit frivolously from my parent's lodging plight, I was even asked to make a student donation! Clearly, 't was the night before graduation and revenge Guy Stevens' style was in order. For the record, revenge is not only sweet, in certain situations it is also much underrated.

Our highly esteemed college president held a reception to meet the parents, kiss babies and have photos taken, just as a shrewd politician should. Each parent also received a glass of Kool Aide and a cookie, in addition to the presidential handshake. How nice…NOT!

I sneaked in line with all the parents and waited for MY TURN to shake the president's hand. As I shook his hand I let out: "Mr. President, so glad to finally meet you. After having attended your fine establishment for four years, this is the first time I have ever seen you. I am so glad you finally made it out of your office to mingle with the commoners."

Mind you, this was not the climax of my little prank! The best part was not only watching the president turn white as a sheet of paper, but seeing the parents and alumni give the man a scathing look. Gone were the looks of admiration and potential alumni generosity. In their place were nasty stares that could ruin the best of political aspirations. Our normally eloquent president suddenly developed a speech impediment as he stammered a lame response: "I, I, I … was here."

Before hundreds of parents and alumni I had put the screws to a $150,000 a year bureaucrat. I reduced him to a stammering moron. No spin control could possibly rescue him from this public relations fiasco.

The moral to this little tale? DON'T MESS WITH GUY STEVENS! Because, in the end, he will get even. Not to mention write a tell-all book about it. Thank you, Mr. College President!

CONTACTING ME

Unlike other (famous) authors, I actually want to hear from you, my readers. If you have a funny story to tell, a piece of advice to pass along, or just want to vent, feel free to contact me. I'd be happy to lend a sympathetic ear. Remember, I have been where you are right now! Thanks for purchasing my book. Feel free to pass it along to your friends.
Fax # 781 - 785- 4000 Check out my website: www.recoveringcollegestudent.com

APPENDIX A
QUICK CHECKLIST

LINENS AND TOWELS

Mattress cover, safety pins
Sheets – fitted bottom, flat top sheet, pillow case
Pillow
Blankets
Towels – three sets and a face cloth

PERSONAL HYGIENE

SHOWER NEED

Bathrobe
Shower bucket
Soap Box
Thong sandals

CLEANSERS

Soap, body wash

HAIR CARE

Shampoo
Hair conditioner
Hairbrush, comb, barrettes, rubber bands, hair bow,etc.
Styling gel, mousse, hair spray
Curling iron

ORAL HYGIENE

Toothbrush, Toothpaste, Dental Floss, Mouthwash

MISCELLANEOUS

Nail file and/or emery boards
Clippers (nail and toenail), tweezers
Nail brush
Moisurizers and body creams
Razor, razor blades
Shaving cream
Styptic Pencil
Aftershave
Makeup – cosmetics, makeup remover, skin lotion, etc.

CLOTHING

UNDERGARMENTS

T-shirts
Bras
Panties
Boxer shorts, briefs
Socks

CASUAL WEAR - WARM CLIMATE

T-Shirt
Shorts
Sneakers
Sandals

CASUAL WEAR - COLD CLIMATE

Sweatshirts
Jeans
Stocking hats
Gloves, mittens
Boots
Scarves
Parkas
Thermal undergarments
Work boots

TELEPHONE

Telephone, answering machine, cordless

BOOKS

Thesaurus
Dictionary

LIGHTS

Desk lamp, reading lamp

SLEEP-RELATED ITEMS

Alarm clock
Ear plugs

STATIONARY SUPPLIES

Pens, Pencils
Eraser
Post It Notes
Blank paper
Envelopes, stamps
Scotch tape
Fun Tack
Ruler
Thumbtacks
Staples, stapler
Glue stick
Calendar, pocket planner
Calculator

HEALTH SUPPLIES

Bandages
Antisepctic cream or ointment
Antacid
Petobismo
Aspirin
Any prescription medication you may be taking
Foot powder
Vitamins
Cough syrup
Sun block
Lip balm
Facial tissues
Cotton balls
Retainers and mouth guard
Skin lotion
Q-Tips
Contraceptives
Wash'n'Drys

LAUNDRY SUPPLIES

Laundry Detergent
Laundry Bags
Laundry Basket
Mini ironing board and iron
Antistatic sheets
Lint remover
Stain remove

APPLIANCES

Refrigerator, Microwave

MISCELLANEOUS

Carpeting
Milk crates
Trunk
Tool box
Fan
Paper towels
Paper plates
Air freshener
Compact disk holder
Can opener
Bottle opener
Backpack

ENTERTAINMENT - FUN STUFF

TV
VCR
DVD
Stereo
Video Games
Baseball bat, glove, ball
Rollerblades

Playing cards
Board games
water pistols

LaVergne, TN USA
14 January 2011
212492LV00001B/6/A

9 780966 412215